EMPTINESS DANCING

Selected Dharma Talks of
ADYASHANTI

Open Gate Publishing
Los Gatos, California

ACKNOWLEDGMENTS

Heartfelt acknowledgment to the following people who contributed to the creation of this book:

Editing: Bonnie Greenwell, Marjorie Bair, Prema Maja Rode. *Proofreading:* Barbara Benjamin, Dwight Lucky, Tara Lucky, Priya Irene Baker, Alison Gause, Gail Galanis, Ed West, Barbara Glinn, Gary Myers. *Editorial Assistance:* Dorothy Hunt, Stephan Bodian, Eric Schneider, Gary Wolf, Jenny Stitz, Shannon Dickson, Jerilyn Munyon. *Audio Recording:* Larry Gray, Peter Scarsdale, Nancy Lowe, Charlie Murphy. *Transcribing:* Hamsa Hilker, Rosanna Sun, Kamala Kadley, Marna Caballero, Dorothy Hunt, Valerie Sher, Peter Humber, Michael Coulter, Annie Gray. *Volunteer Management:* Pralaya. *Legal Counsel:* Gary Wolf. *Graphic Contributions:* Susan Kurtz, Diane Kaye, Rita Bottari, Wil Nolan. *Interior Book Design:* Prema Maja Rode.

And a special thanks to all the volunteers and participants at the events in which the talks in this book were recorded.

ISBN: 0-9717036-4-7

Cover design and photo by Susan Kurtz: susankurtzgraphics.com
Back cover photo of Adyashanti courtesy of Diane Kaye: dianekaye.com
Photo on page xv courtesy of Rita Bottari.
Illustration on page 142 by Wil Nolan: (707) 291-3404

Open Gate Publishing*
P.O. Box 782, Los Gatos, CA 95031, USA
www.zen-satsang.org

*Open Gate Publishing is a division of Open Gate Sangha, Inc.

In loving dedication to my parents,
Larry and Carol Gray.
Thanks for showing me how to laugh.

CONTENTS

INTRODUCTION

By Bonnie Greenwell, Editor

∾

Love moves without an agenda.
It just moves because that is its nature—to move.

These words of spiritual teacher Adyashanti express the essence of his meetings with students when he speaks about the nature of spiritual awakening at weekly gatherings, weekend intensive seminars, and silent retreats. This book is a collection of some of these remarkable talks, selected because they represent consistent and meaningful themes that have been important to his students.

"The heart of what I do, and the heart of what brings you here, is to have the direct experience of who you are," Adyashanti says. "How can you know enlightenment if you don't even know what you are?" In his unique transmission of Truth and freedom, he provides the pointers that can lead students into this discovery, the realization of their true nature.

About Adyashanti

Adyashanti was born in 1962 in Cupertino, California, a small city in the San Francisco Bay area, and was given the name Stephen Gray. It is clear from some of the stories he shares that he enjoyed his childhood and his colorful, extended family, which included two sisters, four grandparents, and an assortment of other relatives. One grandfather enjoyed doing dances of Native American blessing for him and his cousins when they came to visit. He loved bicycle racing as a teenager and young adult, but at age 19, he came across the word "enlightenment" in a book, and was overcome by a fierce hunger to know ultimate Truth. He began training under the guidance of two teachers, Arvis Justi, a disciple of Taizan Maezumi Roshi, and Jakusho Kwong Roshi, a disciple of Suzuki Roshi.

Adyashanti practiced Zen meditation intensely for nearly 15 years, and says he was nearly driven to desperation before he finally awakened into a series of profound realizations about his true nature and experienced the dissolution of attachment to any personal identity. In 1996 he was invited to teach the dharma by his teacher, Arvis Justi. What began as very small group gatherings grew in a few years to weekly dharma talks with hundreds of students. "Dharma" is the word used in Buddhism for the expression of ultimate truth—the underlying nature of all physical and mental phenomena and the true spiritual destiny of all beings. Dharma talks are the teachings offered by one who lives in this truth and has clear realization that has been acknowledged through a lineage of teachers going all the way back to the Buddha.

A slim and graceful man with a shaven head, Adya (as he is called by his students) has a warm presence and a tremendous gift for relatedness and clarity. Students find that the steady gaze of his large and nearly transparent, light blue eyes often disarms the mind and seems to penetrate the heart. Adya's teaching style is heartfelt and direct, free of Zen jargon, but rich with pointers toward universal truth. In the years since that first teaching, many of his students have experienced awakenings through the revelations of his teachings and the transmission that permeates his satsang sessions and retreats.

An Extraordinary Teacher

Adya's style of dharma teaching (also known as "satsang") has been compared to some of the early Chan (Zen) masters of China, as well as teachers of Advaita Vedanta (nondualism) in India. He has a great affinity for the late Advaitic sage, Nisargadatta Maharaj, and other awakened teachers in both Eastern and Western traditions. Although the retreats he leads for students are a blend of silent meditation, dharma talks, and dialogues with students, his approach to awakening is not based on developing spiritual practices, but rather on the disarming and deconstruction of the personal identity.

As have many of his students, I experienced a powerful awakening in Adyashanti's presence, which convinced me that he was my teacher, although I had given up the concept and the search for a teacher years before we met. I then discovered how a teacher/guide can point the cluttered mind toward the exit door and open the heart directly into the love and radiant emptiness that underlies existence.

This is an experience that is extraordinary, profound, and unspeakable; it annihilates all further interest in spiritual seeking and leaves those who know it connected to an interior place that is remarkably simple, quiet, and open. I had been a serious student of Eastern spiritual teachings in several traditions and a teacher and therapist for those who were in the spiritual process, and yet I never clearly saw the power of this extraordinary teacher-student relationship until I discovered *this* teacher, the teacher who was resonant for me. I feel tremendous gratitude for this fortunate meeting.

Adya expresses both the infinite possibilities and the ordinary simplicity of a spiritually-realized life. I experience him as living in the fullness of emptiness and freedom and demonstrating the dynamic relationship between source and spontaneity, heart and humor, and appreciation for the form and the formless aspects of existence.

The Teachings in This Book

This collection of Adya's teachings is culled from hundreds of dharma talks he gave between 1996 and 2002 during satsang meetings, weekend intensives, and retreats. It is being made available so that the pointers, the love, and the transmission he offers can be a continual reminder for his students and also reach many people who are unable to be with him in person.

These talks were chosen because they encompass the initial issues and themes that arise when individuals explore the nature of awakening, liberation, and embodiment with an enlightened teacher. They also describe some of the direct experiences of Adyashanti's awakening and show the world of experience that opens for one who is self-realized: qualities such as innocence, openness, love, impermanence, harmony, peace, depth, and freedom. His words, which are a delightful reflection of the truth that arises from profound inner silence, resonate with our hearts because they express what we really are. They are truth speaking to truth, source revealing its mystery to source.

This resonance has the power to disrupt our habitual patterns of thought and emotional reactivity and help to dismantle the egoic trance, giving us glimpses of the underlying reality of our lives. Such perceptions can literally turn our world upside down, shaking us free from the delusions of mind. Such an opening reveals an entirely fresh way of being alive, vibrant, and free. This aliveness is demonstrated in the expression and the life of this teacher and many of his students.

None of us know how to influence events, however hard we try. In our worldly life, this causes both pain and surprise. But in spiritual life it becomes our grace. When we are able to rest in the not-knowing that is the deep truth of our being in every moment, we allow that which is spontaneous to arise and awaken us. Adya repeatedly tells his students not to hold any concepts, not to believe anything he says to them, and not to cling to any experience.

Spiritual teachings can soothe the mind and bring intellectual understanding, but when awakeness moves through a true teacher's words and being, that awakeness itself may stimulate fire in the heart and focus consciousness in the direction of Self-realization. Ultimately each of us must go within and find our own direct connection with Truth. A teacher can offer pointers and tools for the journey and, through his or her presence, stimulate the inward flow. But in the final act, everything leads to becoming conceptually empty-handed and directionless. You are the way, and the way moves, totally dedicated to revealing itself. It will awaken you to your true nature. Sitting in silence, one needs to do nothing, but rather to allow the natural awakeness to arise. The authentic teacher is one who knows this thoroughly. Living this truth brings the end of suffering.

A Community Offering

The Buddha (all that exists), the Dharma (life truths or teachings), and the Sangha (spiritual community) are called the Three Refuges in Buddhist tradition, which are said to support the transformational process of spiritual realization. A teacher can provide the living presence of truth and can offer the teachings, but cannot provide the community, nor do all the work required to support dozens of gatherings and retreats for students during the year.

A sangha is developing around Adyashanti as his work grows, and many others discover their own capacity for freedom. He has described his relationship to this sangha to be like riding on the caboose of a train, wondering where it is going next because he has set no structured goals or intentions. Awakeness or spirit simply responds through him to whatever arises in the community.

Many dedicated people spent hundreds of hours recording and transcribing the tapes selected for this book, producing and mailing thousands of newsletters and books, organizing and hosting events, answering phones and e-mails, and performing the myriad of tasks that form the backdrop of Open Gate Sangha as a nonprofit organization.

This book rests on the shoulders of those who have done this dedicated work and could not have come into existence without them. I am especially grateful for the many people who have taped and transcribed these meetings and for those who reviewed and made editing suggestions: Marjorie Bair, who donated many hours of her extensive professional editorial expertise; Dorothy Hunt and Stephan Bodian, who provided early editing guidance; and Prema, the designer of this volume, who was the foundation of the Open Gate Sangha staff for four years and now works as the Creative Director overseeing the publication of Adyashanti's many tape sets, books, and other media.

I wish to thank all of the amazing individuals who work on the staff of Open Gate Sangha, the hundreds of volunteers who assist them, and especially Adya's wife, Annie. These people have built and nurtured a solid and responsive base for this community which has allowed for awakening and truth to expand itself in the world around us. I am grateful they have touched my life for many reasons, but especially happy because I was able to do this work of compiling and editing as a service to the truth and in a community where I knew it would be valued, nurtured, and sustained. It is our gift as one community to itself and to the wider community of awakening minds and hearts everywhere. It is our emptiness dancing in the vast openness of the source in order to awaken all of itself.

CHAPTER ONE

AWAKENING

The aim of my teaching is enlightenment—awakening from the dream state of separateness to the reality of the One. In short, my teaching is focused on realizing what you are. You may find other elements in my teaching which simply arise as a response to people's particular needs of the moment, but fundamentally I'm only interested in you waking up.

Enlightenment means waking up to what you truly are and then being that. Realize and be, realize and be. Realization alone is not enough. The completion of Self realization is to be, which means to act, do, and express what you realize. This is a very deep matter, a whole new way of life—living in and as reality instead of living out the programmed ideas, beliefs, and impulses of your dreaming mind.

The truth is that you already are what you are seeking. You are looking for God with his eyes. This truth is so simple and shocking, so radical and taboo that it is easy to miss among your flurry of seeking. You may have heard what I am saying in the past and you may even believe it, but my question is, have you realized it with your whole being? Are you living it?

My speaking is meant to shake you awake, not to tell you how to dream better. You know how to dream better. Depending on what your mental and emotional state at the time is, I may be very gentle and soft with you, or not so gentle and soft. You may feel better after talking with me, but that is incidental to awakening. Wake up! You are all living Buddhas. You are the divine emptiness, the infinite no-thing. This I know because I am what you are, and you are what I am. Let go of all ideas and images in your mind, they come and go and aren't even generated by you. So why pay so much attention to your imagination when reality is for the realizing right now?

Now don't think that awakening is the end. Awakening is the end of seeking, the end of the seeker, but it is the beginning of a life lived from your true nature. That's a whole other discovery—life lived from oneness. Embodying what you are; being a human expression of oneness. There is no question of you becoming the One; you *are* the One. The question is, are you a *conscious* expression of the One? Has the One awakened to itself? Have you remembered what you really are? And if you have, are you living it? Are you really living consciously as the One?

All my talks are about awakening or life lived after awakening. No matter what I *seem* to be talking about, I'm really talking about one of these two things.

∾

Before I had my final awakening years ago, I was crazed for enlightenment. You have to be a little crazy to seriously study Zen. My teacher used to say, "Only the crazy ones stay." One way my craziness worked was that before I went to sit with my teacher's group for a couple of hours on Sunday mornings, I would get up early, at 5:00 or 5:30 a.m., and do extra sittings. I would sit in a little room meditating and freezing to death.

Sitting there on one of those particular mornings, two things happened, one after another, and they seemed very paradoxical. The first one was a spontaneous seeing that everything was one. For me that manifested as hearing a birdcall, a chirp, in the front yard, and from somewhere inside me the question arose, "What is it that hears the sound?" I had never asked this question before. I suddenly realized I was as much the sound and the bird as the one hearing the bird, that the hearing and sound and bird were all manifestations of one thing. I cannot say what that one thing is, except to say *one* thing.

I opened my eyes, and I found the same thing was happening in the room—the wall and the one seeing the wall were the same thing. I thought that was very strange, and I realized that the one thinking this was another manifestation of that. I got up and began to move around the house looking for something that wasn't part of the One. But everything was a reflection of that One thing. Everything was the divine. I wandered into the living room. In the middle of a step, consciousness, or awareness, suddenly left everything, whether it was a physical thing or body thing or world thing.

All in the step of a foot, everything disappeared. What arose was an image of what seemed like an infinite number of past incarnations, as if heads were lined up one behind another as far back as I could see. Awareness realized something like, "My God, I've been identified with various forms for umpteen lifetimes." At that moment, consciousness—spirit—realized it had been so identified with all these forms that it really thought it was a form right up to this lifetime.

All of a sudden, consciousness was unconfined to the form and existed independently. It was no longer defining itself by any form, whether that form was a body, a mind, a lifetime, a single thought, or a memory. I saw this, but I almost couldn't believe it. It was like someone just stuck a million dollars in my pocket, and I kept pulling it out as if I didn't believe I had it. But it couldn't be denied either. Even though I am using the word "I," there was no "I," only the One.

These two experiences happened together, one following within a few moments of the other. In the first, I became the Oneness of everything, and in the second, I became the consciousness or spirit that totally woke up out of all identification, even out of Oneness. When the Oneness dropped away, there was still a basic awakeness, but it had two different aspects: I'm everything, and I'm absolutely nothing. This was the awakening, the realization of Self.

The next thing that happened was that I took a step, just an ordinary step. It felt like the way a baby does when it takes his first good step and then smiles and looks around as if to say, "Did you see that?" and you can see his joy. So I took a step, and it was like, "Wow! The first step!" and another step, and then another, and I kept moving in circles because every step was the first step. It was a miracle.

In each "first" step, formless consciousness and Oneness just merged together so that the awakeness that had always identified itself as form was now actually inside of the form, unidentified. It wasn't looking through any thoughts or memories of what had come before, just through the five senses. With no history or memory, every step felt like a first step.

Then the funniest thought came through my mind— funny to me after 13 years of Zen practice—"Oops. I just woke up out of Zen!" When you wake up, you realize that you wake up out of everything, including all the things that have helped to bring you there. The next thing I did was write my wife this odd note. It said something like, "Happy birthday. Today is my birthday. I've just been born." I left it for her, and when I drove past our house to go to my meditation group, I saw her standing there waving the note in her hand. I don't know how, but she knew exactly what it meant.

I didn't tell my teacher anything about the experience for about three months because it seemed pointless. Why would anyone need to know this? I felt no need to tell anyone or be congratulated. It seemed totally sufficient in and of itself. It was only later that I learned that my experience corresponded to what my teacher had been talking about all along. I realized that this awakening was what all the teachings were about. In a very real way, that experience, which continues and is still the same today, is the foundation of everything I talk about.

When we really start to take a look at who we think we are, we become very grace-prone. We start to see that while we may have various thoughts, beliefs, and identities, they do not individually or collectively tell us who we are. A mystery presents itself: we realize that when we really look at ourselves clearly and carefully, it is actually astounding how completely we humans define ourselves by the content of our minds, feelings, and history. Many forms of spirituality try to get rid of thoughts, feelings, and memories—to make the mind blank, as if that were a desirable or spiritual state. But to have the mind blank is not necessarily wise. Instead, it is more helpful to see *through* thoughts and to recognize that a thought is just a thought, a belief, a memory. Then we can stop binding consciousness or spirit to our thoughts and mental states.

With that first step, when I realized that what was looking through my eyes and senses was awakeness or spirit rather than conditioning or memory, I saw that the same spirit was actually looking through all the other pairs of eyes. It didn't matter if it was looking through other conditioning; it was the exact same thing. It was seeing itself everywhere, not only in the eyes, but also in the trees, the rocks, and the floor.

It is paradoxical that the more this spirit or consciousness starts to taste itself, not as a thought or idea or belief, but as just a simple presence of awakeness, the more this awakeness is reflected everywhere. The more we wake up out of bodies and minds and identities, the more we see that bodies and minds are actually just manifestations of that same spirit, that same presence. The more we realize that who we are is totally outside of time, outside of the world, and outside of everything that happens, the more we realize that this same presence *is* the world—all that is happening and all that exists. It is like two sides of a coin.

The biggest barrier to awakening is the belief that it is something rare. When this barrier is dropped, or at least you start to tell yourself, "I really don't know if my belief that awakening is difficult is true or not," then everything becomes instantly available to you. Since this is all that exists, it can't be rare and difficult unless we insist it is. The basis of all this is not theoretical, it is experiential. No one taught it to me, and no one can teach it to you.

What is so beautiful about awakening is that when you are no longer functioning through your conditioning, then the sense of "me" who was living that life is no longer there. Most people are familiar with the sense of a me living this life. But when this is seen through, the experience is that what really runs and operates this life is love, and this same love is in everybody all the time. When it is working its way through your personal stuff, it gets dissipated, but it is still there. Nobody owns this love. *Everybody* is essentially the manifestation of this love.

You have experienced moments in your life, whether or not you are aware of them, when you momentarily forgot the "I" with which you have been identified. It can happen spontaneously at a beautiful sight, or it can occur from egoic forgetfulness. People usually discount these moments. After experiencing the "nice moment," you then reconstitute your familiar sense of identity. But actually these opportunities are like little peepholes through which the truth is experienced. If you start to watch for them, you will notice them. All of a sudden the mind will stop thinking of its story. You might notice that your separate identity or sense of a me just took a break, and whatever you truly are didn't disappear. Then ask yourself, "What is the real me? If my identity can take a break and I don't disappear, what am I then?" or rather, "What am I when I *do* disappear?"

Usually the mind gets activated in response to the question, "What am I?" It starts thinking about it until true intelligence breaks in again and says, "Now wait a minute—that's just more thought." Then there can be a gap of quietness between thoughts, and if you are very present in that gap, you stop acting out your familiar identity. As soon as identity jumps into the gap, you don't feel present anymore. Being nobody is usually so baffling to the mind that it starts filling that gap very quickly. "How can I be nobody?" But to fill it up with a somebody is meaningless. If you really want to know what you are, just experience the gap, experience the openness, and let it bloom inside. There is no better way to find out what you are.

This is when spirituality becomes not only real, but adventurous and fun. You ask, "This openness, this presence"—call it what you will—"this is what I am?" You start to feel or sense that you're on to something that's not a creation of thought, belief, or faith. And when you start to take it in, just this awakeness that's free of all identity, it's mind-boggling. In Zen we call it the uncreated; it's the only thing around that your mind is not creating.

There is a wonderful parable from the Bible that says it is easier for a camel to pass through the eye of a needle than for a rich man to get into heaven. Trying to hold on to your identities, even if they are the most spiritual, most holy of identities, is like trying to shove a camel through the eye of a needle. They are too coarse, too big, too untrue, too fabricated to get into the truth. But there's one thing that can get through the eye of the smallest possible needle. Space, your own nothingness, can get right through into heaven. None of us can take one shred of a self-centered identity with us.

Heaven is the experience when we've passed into our own nothingness. We realize our own pure awakeness and see that what we are is pure spirit with no form. We recognize that formless spirit is the essence, the animating presence of everything. This is being in heaven because, in each step, spirit and essence are occupying our body. That's the true meaning of being born again. Being born again is not just a great emotional religious conversion experience. That can be nice, but it's only like changing your clothes. Being born again is actually being born *again*, not getting a new spiritual garment. More accurately, it is being *unborn* when we realize that eternal nothingness is actually living this life called "my life."

But just because you realize the truth and awaken spiritually, doesn't mean that your life is going to be an unending ascent of good fortune. That would not be the peace that surpasses all understanding. As long as our lives feel good, it is easy to have peace. But life does what it does, like an ocean moving. Whether the waves are high or low, it is just as sacred and, as nobody, you are not harmed by it. Within this awakeness is the peace that surpasses understanding, and your life doesn't need to be doing better. It can just do what life does; it just flows. You don't care.

~

Student: Letting go of our egocentricity so we can experience awakening—do you suppose it is peeled off us the way we peel an orange?

Adyashanti: Peeling is like having a dream at night in which you dream you are going to a therapist, and you start feeling better and better, and you feel like you are getting somewhere. Awakening is as if you are sitting on the couch telling your story, and you are still a mess—haven't gotten very far. Then all of a sudden you realize this is a dream, this isn't real, you're making it up. That's awakening. There's a big difference.

Student: I've made up all of it?

Adyashanti: The whole thing. But the awakeness in you is not dreaming. Only the mind is dreaming. It tells itself stories and wants to know if you're progressing. When you shift into wakefulness, you realize, "Wait, it's a dream. The mind is creating an altered state of reality, a virtual reality, but it's not true—it's just thought." Thought can tell a million stories inside of awareness, and it's not going to change awareness one bit. The only thing that's going to change is the way the body feels. If you tell yourself a sad story, the body reacts to that. And if you tell yourself a self-aggrandizing story, the body feels puffed up, confident. But when you realize it's all stories, there can be a vast waking up out of the mind, out of the dream. *You* don't awaken, what has eternally been awake realizes *itself*. That which is eternally awake is what you are.

Berkeley, California: December 9, 2001

CHAPTER TWO

SATSANG

We meet here to recognize the Truth that is eternal. To be in *satsang* means to be in association with Truth. When we understand this, we can meet here together with a common intention.

When you come to satsang to have association with Truth, you are willing to ask, "Who am I?" or "What am I?" without any script or role, without the story about who you are and what you are, releasing the script of what you think your life is about. Every sense of identity has its script. Some of the roles in those scripts might be, "I'm the successful guy or girl," or "I'm the unsuccessful one," or "I'm the one whose relationships never work out," or "I'm the spiritual seeker who has had many spiritual experiences." We each have a specific role and our stories about that role. But our roles and stories are not what we are.

The beautiful thing about satsang is that it's an opportunity to wake up from the story of you. When you start to realize what Truth is, you recognize that Truth is not an abstraction, it is not out there at a distance from you, and it is not something to learn tomorrow. You discover that Truth is who you are without your story or script, right now.

The real blessing of this meeting is the opportunity to be stopped right now, not tomorrow. Awakening to the truth of your being won't be attained in the future. It's not something you prepare for or earn or deserve. Awakening is a radical shift in identity. You think you're you, but you're not. You are eternal being. The time to wake up is now. Not tomorrow. Now.

When the little me starts to realize why it is here in satsang, it thinks, "This can't be a place for me. I thought I had come here to gain an advantage, but there is none." It's a revolutionary idea for any of us to go anywhere or do anything where we wouldn't be gaining an advantage. It's not that there is anything wrong with getting an advantage at times. But in satsang, what we come to see is that our happiness and freedom have nothing to do with gaining any sort of advantage. Instead, they have everything to do with allowing ourselves to experience in this moment what it's like to be completely disarmed of our strategy. That includes our strategy to be rid of strategy. This is an opportunity to stop all strategies of becoming.

The blessing here is that we are welcoming the direct experience of the little me being disarmed. Almost everywhere else you go, that sense of being disarmed is

pushed away, hidden, not even talked about or acknowledged. Here we can ask, instead, "What am I, and who
am I *now*—without my story, without my demand upon
this moment, without my hope of this moment, without
my script?" The mind, if it were to say anything, would
answer, "I don't know," because the mind does not know
what it is when it's disarmed, it doesn't know who or what
it is without its role or its character to play.

The actor who is acting all this out is named "me." Even
when we respond to or welcome the call of satsang, that
actor keeps maintaining himself or herself, and the
tendency of mind is to say, "I'm here." But when we look
for what is behind the "I'm here," it's like yelling in an
empty room—there's an echo, "I'm here," and every time
we look, we find only an echo. Who? "I'm here." Who?

So then you start to let go even more, to be disarmed
from engaging in the more subtle game of thinking you
are an actor behind the role. You start to see that that is
just another narrative. If you truly look, there is the
wonderful chance to be fully disarmed because you will
not find an actor, or anyone at all.

When this disarming happens, you are allowing the
wordless experience to present itself. This is the wordless
experience of *being* that you can experience for yourself.
You will realize that it is not a script or role, it carries no
agenda, and has no demand upon this moment. It's also
not the actor. What you are is prior to your idea of you.

What you are without your role is often assumed to be hidden somewhere. And so when you let go of your role, when you look past the character called "me" for the truth of your being, you may think that there's a someone to find who is somehow hidden. If this happens, when you come into this state of openness, you may think, "There's nobody here, but I'll look for it anyway, look for the Self, the Truth, the enlightened me." Looking for the enlightened self is just another role, another script. It's part of the spiritual seeker's script. If you drop that script—*now* what are you?

Of course, the reason I ask you to inquire into what you are is because, at this moment, you are living the answer. Nothing that I would tell you is a substitute for that aliveness, for that living of the answer. That's why it has been said many times that only the people who don't know who they are, are the ones who are awake. Everyone else knows who he or she is. They are their script, whatever their script is, even if that script is, "I'm not awake." Awakeness is to have *no* script, to know that ultimately a script is just a script, and a story is just a story.

There is a state in which the mind says, "I have no idea who I am," because it can't find the right script. Awakening is the realization that happens after the mind says, "I give up. I just have no idea who I am." When you start to understand this, you realize that if you put down your script of being someone listening, and if you put down your script of being someone saying something, and you just drop these roles for a moment, you are not who you have taken yourself to be. Coming to satsang is a very revolutionary thing for this idea of "me" to do, because the me thinks it's going to get its happiness through changing its script, its role, its identity—even if its identity is to have no identity. It will do whatever it takes to keep the ball called "me" rolling.

Our spiritual culture has become very tricky. We have increasingly subtle spiritual concepts to use in our discussions. Many people have replaced the old heavy concept of God and sin with the words consciousness and conditioning, which sound a little lighter. The modern spiritual person has these extremely abstract concepts. The more abstract the concept, the more transparent it is. It's hard to make an image of consciousness and put it on your altar. Your altar keeps being emptied. If you want to see the Truth, don't put anything there. The best altar of all would have nothing on it.

Even abstract concepts, though, if you identify with them, can catch you and prevent the mind from being disarmed. Even when there is a sudden experience of awakeness it is very easy for the mind to come into this living spirit of awakeness, put its stamp on it, and make it a something: "This is awakeness, or awareness, or consciousness, or Self." The mind will call it anything just so it will not be disarmed. So we see that even the most sacred concept, if it is not held very lightly, can become a subtle defense against this present state of *being* which cannot be fixated in concept.

If we ask, "Who am I without the me-concept? What am I without the me?" instantly the wordless can open up, the concept-less can open up. Allow the *experience* of that, because that is the *living* answer to the questions, "What am I? Who am I?" This is not the dead conceptual answer, but the living answer. It is alive! In this moment of radiant awakeness there's a mystery unfolding unto itself, moment to moment to moment. This living state of being, call it what you will, is the only thing that you always have been, always will be, and are right now. You are not a human being, you are *being* appearing as human.

True inquiry is like a childlike wondering, "Is this really who I am?" Not thinking about it, but allowing yourself to be more and more disarmed through the question. The more sincerely you experientially enter the unknown, the more you become disarmed. Have you noticed the mind doesn't know what to do? Invite that sense of unknowing, and do not be concerned about being disarmed. Notice that right in the middle of it there is a vivid, radiant awakeness. Mysteriously, by allowing the recognition of that awakeness in, you can awaken as that.

When you allow awakeness in, you will find that it plays games with your life. It doesn't move according to the agenda of the little me, the one who has all these ideas about this or that happening when you awaken. The awakeness could care less about the agendas you have. It's moving, and it's not listening to what you want, and you are grateful that it's not listening. You discover that it has its own movement, which I suppose is what real surrender is—following that movement. This is the real meaning of "Thy will be done."

The mind may get concerned about being disarmed and letting go of all its concepts and scripts. It might say, "I may not get what I want." And I say, you're damned lucky if you don't get what you want! I got nothing I wanted out of awakening. I thought it would solve lots of things. I had lots of ideas about what it was going to give me. Forget it! Not that you don't get what you want, but you don't *care* if you get what you want. I can't think of one thing I got that I thought I would get. The only thing that did happen was that I no longer cared. What a hideous dream it was—thinking those things were needed for me to be happy.

To welcome the mystery of your own being is satsang. This is in contrast to what spirituality often is—pushing your own being away, or defining the mystery, or dressing it up with pearls and flowers, etc., so it looks like a powerful mystery. Satsang is a welcoming, such a welcoming, until the identification snaps and the mystery realizes, "Oh, this is what I am! I thought I was the one over there with that agenda. I thought I was the actor of roles. I thought I *was* the roles." None of that is true. When the role called "I'm a human being" ends, we call that death. It's a lot easier if you let that role die before the body dies, and let it be put to rest now. Through satsang you can awaken to being what you eternally are and have true life.

Santa Cruz, California: June 3, 2001

CHAPTER THREE

OPENNESS

An important part of satsang, when we gather together to explore Truth, is being open-hearted. Some human beings find it easier to be open-minded, and some find it easier to be open-hearted, but to really be here now is to be both. When you are open, you do not filter your experience, nor do you barricade yourself. You do not try to defend yourself, but you open to the mystery by questioning what you believe.

When you give yourself this amazing gift of not trying to find yourself within some particular concept or feeling, then the openness expands until your identity becomes more and more the openness itself, rather than some point of reference in the mind called a belief or a particular feeling in the body. The point is not to get rid of thoughts or feelings, but just not to feel located inside of them.

Openness has no particular location. It seems to be everywhere. It has room for anything. There can be a thought or no thought. There can be a feeling or no feeling.

There can be sounds. There can be silence. Nothing disturbs openness. Nothing disturbs your true nature. We only get disturbed when we close ourselves by identifying with a particular point of view, a concept of who I am or who I believe or feel myself to be; we go into opposition against what's happening. But when we are being our true nature, which is openness, we find that we're actually not in opposition to anything. Whatever is happening in the openness is perfectly okay, and so we are able to respond to life in a spontaneous and wise way.

Satsang is about remembrance. It's as if you forgot you were this openness and thought that you were something. Humans have spun endless mythologies of how we forgot, but it doesn't really matter how. The heart of satsang is not to change and alter yourself, but to remember what you are. Truth is about just remembering, recognizing, or realizing your true nature.

Do you know the experience of forgetting something even though it was right there in your mind a moment ago? The mind may struggle to remember, but this just makes it more difficult. What finally helps? You relax a little bit. You forget that you're trying to remember, and you relax. "Oh yes, that's it!" The answer comes out of nowhere. Self-realization is just like that—just now. It happens in the willingness to relax and not know.

You can have an experience of openness right now. You do not need to open or to become more open. Just recognize the openness that is already being experienced here and now. This is known inside, outside, and everywhere. Just feel the experience of it. Let go of the word "openness." Let it disappear, and the experience gets deeper and becomes more and more wordless. Simply *be* from the place that is wordless. Then you are not confused by words, and you do not limit your experience by believing in the words. But as soon as you impose the word "openness," your experience takes on a certain flavor, which isn't quite right. It may be very close, but it is not quite what it was when you didn't have the concept.

This letting go can deepen. That deepening may seem like falling into the unknown to the mind, which tends to conceptualize it and limit the experience, but it's actually a deeper knowing of the experience of *being* itself. In that deeper experience, the limited person you thought you were starts to realize that you are this openness instead. You will also see that this is what others are. When you liberate yourself, it's not just your self, it is *the* Self that is liberated. You're remembering everybody's Self because it's the same Self. When this is realized, it enables the total transformation of human interaction.

Open mind, open heart. Realize that there isn't somebody in there to protect. There is no need for an emotional barrier or the feelings of separation and isolation that come from that barrier. The only reason you ever thought that you needed protection was because of a very innocent misunderstanding. This happened because when you were given a concept of yourself in very early childhood, you also received a kit with which to build walls that would protect this concept. You learned to add to the kit as circumstances arose. If a good dose of anger seemed useful, you would add that to the kit, or perhaps you added resentment, shame, blame, or victimization. Whether you cling to a self-image as a good person or an inadequate person, the kit of identity is used to protect that image.

This is very innocent. It happens without your knowing that it's happening. It continues until you realize that inherent in this holding of "me" as a self-image in the mind and body is the belief that you need protection. You can't have one without the other. They come in the same box.

When you drop your protection, the truth comes in and takes away the self-image. That's why the self-image came with a wall because, without the wall, the remembrance of your true nature is going to jump in fast and take away the self-image, whether good or bad. There is no self-image that doesn't have a wall and no self-image that doesn't entail suffering. Not only do you have your own walls, but there are also walls you project onto other people, the images you have of them that prevent you from seeing their true nature.

With the willingness to see that an image is not real, the walls come down. When the intellectual wall opens up, you become open-minded. When the emotional wall opens up, you become open-hearted. When realization of the Truth removes the limited me, there is suddenly no self-image—but only total presence. Total presence! This openness is present and imageless. There is no need to protect it. Somebody can yell at it, and sound goes through space. That's okay. Someone can love it. That's nice, but it doesn't add anything to it or subtract anything from it.

Now the funny thing about the Truth, or enlightenment, or awakening, is that we miss it even though it's not hidden. It's not far away waiting for a moment when we deserve it. It is hard to find because it is right here. This openness has always been here. If it had a voice, it would have been saying something like, "For Pete's sake, I wonder how long this image thing is going to go on!"

This imageless Self—call it awakeness or awareness or openness, whatever word might trigger the remembrance for you—is very quiet. But don't believe me. Take the words inside. Discover for yourself. You are the authority. I'm just the messenger.

The more you realize that you are openness, the more your physical body realizes there is nothing to protect. Then it can open itself. On an emotional level, you can feel this as a sensation in your muscles and your bones. Then the body's deepest function starts to unfold, and it becomes an expression of the openness you are in physical form, an expression of truth instead of the protector of the me. It becomes an extension of openness itself. The movement of your hand or your foot becomes an expression of openness; contact with an object feels like an extension of openness. You feel almost an infant-like fascination with movement and your senses and what is present in the world. The difference is that when the spiritual awakening gets deep and matures, you have what the infant is missing: wisdom. The infant, over time, identifies with the objects of its attention and the messages others give it about itself. When the mature body-mind starts to be an extension of the openness, of its true nature, it rediscovers innocence, except now there is a deep wisdom that allows it to be fascinated without ever grasping or pushing anything away, which is unnecessary. So the movement and the fascination are not infantile. They are childlike, but absolutely wise. This openness holds the deepest, deepest wisdom. Then you are finally able to be fascinated without losing yourself in an identity and with no sense that you can be threatened.

The infant's whole world is about the body. This is as it should be, as it needs to be. But the innocent sage is not concerned about sustaining the body. It gets sustained, but not because of fear of not sustaining it. That's why in the re-remembering, in the deepest homecoming to your Self, there is a freedom to actually be here, living this life without fear.

Another aspect of openness is intimacy. The quickest access to Truth, and also to beauty, is when you are totally intimate with all of experience, the inner and the outer, even if the experience isn't "good." When you are being intimate with the whole of experience, the divided mind has to let go of whatever its project is at the moment. In this intimacy, one becomes very open and discovers a vastness. Whether the qualities of the experience are unpleasant or beautiful, as soon as you are intimate with the whole of experience, there is openness.

When there is intimacy with all of the experience of the moment, awareness is not limited to what's happening in your emotional body, your physical body, your perceptions, or your thoughts. There is just one whole perceiving itself, feeling itself, or thinking itself, and whatever is happening tends to resolve itself. When the whole perceives itself, it is very different than when the I is having an experience. When we let go in this way, as Zen Master Bankei used to say, "Everything is perfectly managed in the Unborn." He used the term Unborn for what I call Truth. When the whole perceives itself, there is the impression the Unborn is completely managing itself. It never holds on to experience. It just harmonizes itself and enjoys itself. And when you let go of your project or agenda, it can be seen that everything is perfectly managed in the Unborn.

Sometimes you notice you have some project going on in your mind. You are trying to get rid of something or understand something, and you are thinking about it. Consider giving yourself a break and stop thinking for a moment. Einstein did this. He would think about a problem, and then he would stop thinking about it, believing he had gone as far as he could go and had exhausted the rational thought process. Now it's a trick to do this. Most people find the rational thought process takes them to an edge and, instead of stopping, they take a 90-degree right turn or left turn and start moving along the edge, thinking horizontally, pulling in more facts and experiences and memories. This is called a waste of time. The only use of thought that has power is a rational process that goes right to the edge of thought, and then stops. It lets something else deliver whatever needs to be delivered, much like Einstein did when he took the thinking process to the end and then let it be delivered. Then the Unborn perfectly manages everything just because it is being intimate with experience.

The quickest access to this openness to your true nature is not so much by thinking, but through the five senses. For example, if you listen to the whole moment and not just the sounds available to the ears, if you *feel* the entirety of the whole moment, you will be opened beyond the limited space of the me. There is a particular feeling in your body, and you just feel it—it stretches. You feel the absolute quietness. You feel the birds. You feel what it is like to feel a sound.

The five senses give you immediate access beyond the virtual reality mind, to something that is not mentally created. It is amazing when you start to let your five senses open up. You realize that ninety-nine percent of your problem was that you had everything confined, focused in one direction only, and when you open to the whole, everything becomes very clear. As soon as you start to suffer, you notice that your five senses have given up focusing on the whole and are instead focused on only one thing, which causes suffering.

You can start to see that so much of suffering has happened because this focus on a narrow point of experience makes it very hard for the Unborn to manage itself. But as soon as focus opens, the Unborn is known to be managing itself and everything is okay, even if it seems to be not okay. Then you can move beyond a limited point of view and see that it is not really true that *you* perceive all of these experiences, but rather it is the *whole* that perceives *itself.*

Palo Alto, California: July 25, 2001

CHAPTER FOUR

INNOCENCE

Three qualities arose in me when I experienced a deep awakening: wisdom, innocence, and love. Although they are actually parts of one whole, this wholeness can be expressed by these three qualities.

Awakening opens wisdom. When I speak of wisdom, it doesn't mean that I suddenly became smart. It simply means that I realized the Truth. This Truth is what I am. This is what the world is. This is what *is*. The wisdom is the realization of what you are. It is the realization of Truth, the one and only true truth. This Truth is not a matter of philosophy, or science, or faith, or belief, or religion. It is beyond all of that—far beyond.

The second quality born within this awakening was innocence. This tremendous innocence produces the feeling of an ever-present newness in life. Since the awakening, the brain no longer holds and compares, so every moment is experienced as new, just as it would be in the mind of a young child. The adult mind tends to take things in, compare its perceptions to the litany of things that have happened in the past, and basically hold the attitude, "Been there, done that." It is rather arid, dry, and boring. The innocent mind arises when this comparison is no longer happening. This innocence could also be called humility. But I personally like the word innocence because I think it stays closer to the actual experience.

The third quality that arose was love. This love is simply for existence. What is born in awakening is a love of what *is*—of everything that is. The fact that there is anything at all seems wonderful because when the insight of awakening goes very deep, there is a realization about how tenuous existence is. I don't simply mean that we could be killed at any moment. I mean we see an unbelievable miracle, we see how unimaginably easy it would be for absolutely nothing to be here. (Actually, there is absolutely nothing, but that's another story.) That anything exists at all is seen as an absolute and utter miracle, and from that seeing there is the birth of so much love simply for what is. It's a different love than when we love getting what we want or we find the perfect partner. This is a love just for the fact that we have shoelaces or for the fact that toenails exist, that kind of love. A tremendous love arises simply for the miracle that is life, realizing that all and everything is the One.

When the awakening is very deep, we no longer operate from a place of personal self. In other words, everything doesn't relate to "me." Thoughts don't relate to me, feelings don't relate to me, what others do doesn't relate to me, and what happens in the world doesn't relate to me. In the egoic state of consciousness, literally every single thing that ever happens is happening to a me. Right? That's the "normal" state of consciousness.

Nobody can really explain what the personal self is; we just feel it. It's a visceral thing. It's not just how we act and what we say, it's our central fixation of self. As we see through it, we realize that the personal self is not who we are and that it was not ever anything substantial to begin with. And as we really see into our true nature, there is a paradox that arises: the more we realize that there isn't a self, the more intimately present we actually are.

So, what took the place of the personal self in my experience was the innocence and the love. Of course, they had been there all the time, but they were covered over by this conglomeration of thoughts and feelings that had become "me." This innocence continues to amaze me because it never ends. It continues to be innocent no matter how much it sees, no matter how deep its spiritual insight or its spiritual depth grows, and it continues to grow more innocent. With the egoic sense of self, the more we know, the less innocent we feel. But to our true nature, the more we know, the more innocent we feel.

I call this feeling innocence not only because it has the feeling of innocence with which everyone can identify, but also because it has the sense of being very unguarded. When we are unguarded, we notice that this innocence comes only from itself. Here is a way to understand this: when we relate from the egoic state of consciousness, we are basically coming from an idea, a point of view that is a conglomeration of beliefs or memories. When we are coming from innocence, we are not coming from an idea, a point of view, or a belief. We are coming from innocence itself, which isn't a particular point of view. It doesn't have an ideology; it doesn't have a theology; it doesn't have a list of beliefs; and it doesn't have a list of ideas. It's the only thing in the world that is very sure that it doesn't know what is going on. In innocence, there is no idea about what's going on, and this is the wonderment. When I say it doesn't know what's going on, I mean it's not relating to experience through thought. It's bypassing thought when it relates to experience. It's not being filtered at all. That's why it's innocent.

This aspect of the awakened self, this innocence, is actually present as a taste in every being. For the mind, for the egoic state of consciousness, it may seem like a nice place to visit, but it's a terrifying place to hang out because it takes all the tools of the egoic state of consciousness and renders them useless. The egoic state of consciousness likes to visit this place because it's a nice little relief, like going to the Bahamas for a couple of minutes inside. But the mind is actually not very comfortable staying there because it is nonoperational while it's there. We see that we are not who we thought we were, and the world is not what we thought it was. Everything is new and open and unpredictable, which makes the ego feel insecure.

It can be difficult to understand how thorough this innocence is. For example, if you are sitting in your chair and you have a certain sensation arise in your body that your mind would immediately label fear, the innocence wouldn't know that. Even a feeling the mind would call fear isn't recognized by innocence because it's not perceiving through mind. It would look at it like, "I'll be darned, what is this?" When you become interested in something, you move toward it. If a sound is interesting, you lean into it. If a smell is interesting, you sniff. Innocence just looks with curiosity and asks, "What is it?" And it draws the sensation very close. It discovers what that sensation is through the experience rather than through the idea. It's very different to experience the sensation of fear through experience rather than through the idea of it. Because a word like fear has been passed down through generations— there is a transmission of mind from generation to generation—as soon as the thought comes up in your head that says "fear," it's not just about this moment, it's about countless generations of fear.

But innocence isn't looking through thought so it's bypassing history. It's newly discovering each moment. It's not something that the egoic mind chooses—"Okay, I'm going to be innocent, and I'm going to discover each moment, and I'm going to pay attention." This is to miss it because this makes it into a project for the egoic state of consciousness. The innocence already exists and is approaching and experiencing each moment in a totally innocent way. When you start to touch upon it, you start to feel the childlike curiosity of it; you find that it actually moves toward experience, toward each thing. That's why in many religions there is the advice to be childlike (which is not childish, but childlike) because that childlikeness is always so vitally interested in what is. This is the quality of freshness we feel when we are living from no separate self.

Of course we still have a brain and we still have thoughts, so things are still learned and experiences are accumulated. The egoic state of consciousness always perceives through this accumulated knowledge. The only difference in living from no separate self is that we do not perceive through that accumulation, although we can reach into it when necessary. Perceiving instead through innocence actually makes us extraordinarily capable of being wise in the moment because, in that state, the deepest wisdom of the moment arises. This wisdom belongs only to the moment and is not part of our accumulated knowledge. In Zen we call it *prajna*, heart wisdom, which is a wisdom that belongs to the whole. It belongs to the moment. We no longer relate from the personal sense of me but from the whole of existence.

The other quality that I found in awakening was a love for the mere fact of existence itself. It wasn't a love that was caused by anything. It wasn't based on a good day, or a good person, or a good encounter, or a good feeling. In fact, it could be not such a good day, not such a good encounter, not such a good person, or not such a good feeling, and there was still just as much love for it. This is a love that loves to live this life because in life it is actually meeting itself moment to moment.

Awakening reveals that there is no personal self, and that everything is myself. It appears to be a paradox. We find we are nothing and absolutely everything simultaneously. When we see this, we realize there is nothing more happening other than love meeting itself—or we could say you are meeting yourself, or the Truth is meeting itself, or God is meeting itself. Love meets itself each moment, even if it's a rotten moment. This will never happen through the egoic state of consciousness, filtered through the mind. But from the innocence, love is simply meeting itself. If you love me, it meets that. If you hate me, fine, it meets that, too. And it loves meeting that. I am talking about the One meeting itself, realizing itself, experiencing itself.

This is a love that includes the good feelings that we associate with love, and it also far transcends good feelings. It is a love that's much deeper than an experience. Have you noticed, with whatever quality of love you have experienced, that when true love arises, it opens up both your mind and emotions? It's an openness to whatever is happening. The egoic state of consciousness is always closing the doors. Emotionally and intellectually, it's always slamming things shut as soon as the moment isn't the "right" kind of moment, which is about ninety-nine percent of the time. But the innocence and the love do not slam the door shut, even in the face of something that is very unpleasant.

Notice that the more you see past your sense of personal self, the more innocence creeps in. And the more innocence is known, the more love sticks its head out and starts to experience life, live this life, and move within this life. The wisdom becomes available now because one is open. So the wisdom deepens, and the innocence deepens. And the innocence allows for more love, and the more love there is, the more room there is for wisdom, and so it goes.

These qualities of love and innocence are what make liberating wisdom possible. They are not only outcomes of the blooming of your true nature, they are also what make awakening and the embodiment of it, possible.

Berkeley, California: November 25, 2001

CHAPTER FIVE

HARMONIZATION

In Zen, one of the definitions of enlightenment is the harmonization of body and mind. This also means the harmonization of spirit and matter. When spirit and matter are in harmony, it's as if a third entity is born—that's really the Buddhist "Middle Way." The Middle Way has nothing to do with the notion of being halfway between two opposites. The Middle Way is when spirit and matter are in harmony—when the inherent oneness is realized. Spirit and matter are not two different things, they are two aspects of the One. This is the realization of our true nature.

As humans we become identified with matter. Matter includes every subtle and gross manifestation. Matter is anything that can be touched, seen, felt, perceived, or thought. A feeling is matter and emotion is matter, as is a body, a car, or a floor.

The essence of matter is spirit. Matter is animated by spirit, by the life force, and they cannot be separated. Although we can speak about them as if they are two things, if we take away the life force, there is no matter. It's not as if there is dead matter. There is no matter.

Part of realization is moving from identification with matter (which manifests as personality or "me") to identification with spirit. True enlightenment is when matter and spirit are in harmony. We could call this harmony nondifferentiation or oneness.

When we realize that we are spirit, there may be a much deeper harmony than there was before that realization, but there can still be some disharmony. So it is helpful to understand the value of exposing ourselves to the teaching, which is the same as exposing ourselves to what *is*, each and every moment. We need to expose ourselves as we would to the sun if we want to get a tan. Instead of putting on clothes, we take them off. If we want to be free, then we don't clothe ourselves with our concepts, ideas, and opinions; we take them off. Then something happens quite by itself. In order to deepen this harmony, we cannot hold on to concepts just like we cannot stay partially dressed and get a full tan. We will not get transformed. But once we are really naked and completely exposed, we can become transformed or awakened in a very natural way.

Many years ago one of my two teachers, Kwong Roshi, knew I was going to go out into the mountains backpacking for a few months, so he taught me how to find the right place to stay at night. It's not that he gave me information on how to do it. He just talked about it for a while, and then all of a sudden I realized that I would be able to directly sense the environment that was right for me. Just as we can feel our environments, we can feel when there is a harmonization of spirit and matter in our environments. Those are good environments to hang out in, and they quite naturally harmonize us.

The more harmonization there is, the more there is an intensification of the Truth, or radiance, within us. Of course the radiance is everywhere. We can't get away from it. But for a period of time, it's helpful to have some intensification in our environment. It's useful to have support because we can lose the sense that there is radiance everywhere all the time. As we go deeper, we will experience the radiance everywhere, even if it doesn't appear in a concentrated, potent, or powerful way. We come to that by being willing to expose ourselves to experiences and places that make it more potent.

In every retreat that I hold, I can feel the minute that the retreat as a whole—certain individuals before, certain individuals after—starts to harmonize spirit and matter. When it clicks, some people get happy and some people get scared because it gets more powerful. This harmonization is the reason it's been said that, if you want to wake up, you need to hang around awakened beings. It can be awakened human beings, awakened trees, awakened mountains, awakened rivers—it can be any environment. If we are sensitive, we can feel when environments are awakened. Human beings can be more or less awakened. So can trees or a mountain, canyon, hilltop, or a particular street corner in our neighborhood. When we are sensitive, we can feel these things. When we expose ourselves to that awakeness, to that environment where spirit and matter are harmonized, it helps us awaken. Ultimately, that's what satsang is. That's also what meditation really is. We are exposing ourselves, and then, quite naturally, spirit and matter harmonize. All of a sudden it just clicks, without you doing anything. The less you do the better.

When we relax and allow this natural harmonization, there is a deep awakening to the beauty of our environment, just as it is, and to the beauty of our own selves. That's the Middle Way, but it's not really in the middle, it's all encompassing. This subtle influence can be very strong. It's sneaky, like mist seeping into the cracks and the crevices of our lives. It doesn't like to announce itself with fanfare.

I can remember the day I was doing a retreat with Kwong Roshi, and out of nowhere I realized, "I know what's happening!" Not in my head but inside. That influence, that beauty, started to wake up in me, and I understood something that was unspoken but always available. When I sat and listened to Kwong talk at retreats, sometimes I was very interested so I would really be listening, and at other times it wouldn't be as interesting, so I wouldn't be listening quite as much. As he would say, "Sometimes it's good talk, sometimes it's not so good talk. That's how talk goes." It happened on one of those days when I wasn't listening quite as much to the words. I wasn't away in a fantasy, but I wasn't listening carefully. All of a sudden it was like smoke, that subtle stream of presence was sensed. I knew, "That's what he is doing. It's not about all this talk, talk, talk." I realized that's not what was going on—or it was just a little bit of what was going on. I remember sitting there with a smile thinking how sneaky he was because, for some reason, through no choice of his own or of any of us present, there was a magnification happening of something very subtle but very pervasive.

This way is sneaky because we think nothing is happening. Therefore we are not chasing anything. So I had missed it until that day and that one talk, when I experienced that subtle source, and it was just shining. I saw it and sensed it, and then it was shining inside me, too. It was the same thing inside. I started to see, *this* is what I am! *This* gives life to everything. I felt a perfect, beautiful harmonization of body and mind, spirit and matter. It happened just through exposure. I wouldn't call this true awakening, but it was a foretaste of awakening. Realizing the sacred presence.

Charisma can be very beautiful. But if a teacher is too charismatic, students tend to grasp. They tend to look only at the body and think, "What a wonderful person!" He or she might be a wonderful person, but it's not about a wonderful person. I see it as the greatest gift for me that neither one of my teachers were charismatic personalities. As soon as we move into the worship of the charisma or anything else, we start to unconsciously look past the presence that really is, the presence that can function through strong personalities and also through meek and mild personalities. It can function through great charisma and through almost no charisma. None of us has any choice about that part of it. It can function through the grandmother just as much as it can function through the Divine Mother guru.

When we realize what we are through this harmonization, then what do we do? We keep baking forever. If we stop baking and say, "I got it!" all of a sudden the harmonization of spirit and matter goes out of kilter. It is felt very quickly. As Suzuki Roshi often said, "If you are suffering, you got a little greedy." You need to surrender continually so that harmonization maintains itself.

The old Taoists would call this "rectifying the *chi*." In ancient times, and probably today in a few places, the Taoist priest was called in if there was a problem in the village. If the community was not getting along or there was turmoil of some sort, he or she would be invited. So he would trot off from his hermitage and go to the town and say something like, "Give me a quiet place, give me a cabin, and leave me alone." There he would sit down and open himself to the chi of the environment, to the energy. Now that's a great compassion because when you open yourself to the environment, if it's out of kilter, you are going to feel the out of kilter in your own being. It's all going to happen inside just as it's happening outside. But if you have enough stability, if you have enough insight, nothing in you is going to be worried about that. It's not going to be a problem. It's not even going to make you suffer, but it will just happen: turbulence. Only when you've fully realized yourself, do you have the fearlessness to do that. Otherwise, if you open yourself up, you get totally lost.

The Taoist priest would sit there in the cabin and just open himself to the chi, or the energy of the environment— feel it, experience it, and then open the chi to the light of his own consciousness. It could take a day, a week, sometimes a month, but he'd just expose the chi to the light of his own consciousness and the energy would start to rectify itself. Then people in the village would start to feel better and get along for awhile.

That's why scriptures have advised us to hang out with awakened beings. The awakened one could be a human being, a tree being, a street corner being. Expose yourself to them. Don't worship them and put them on a pedestal. But expose yourself and this rectification happens; this harmonization happens because of their state of consciousness. But don't become dependent. You wake yourself up.

The light of consciousness has no mind to change or alter anything. There is no sense that anything needs to change, but it does change. So the priest could just sit, and all would rectify. Everybody would just feel much better. Of course, not for very long because, if they haven't seen the sun inside themselves, once the awakened consciousness leaves the environment, everyone goes crazy again. But the priest is cool about that. The sun doesn't argue about where it's shining or why it was asked to shine. People awaken and transform only when they truly want to. Until that time all change is temporary. No one can force permanent awakening upon you.

When you start to see the light that you really are, the light waking up in you, the radiance, you realize it has no intention to change you. It has no intention to harmonize. It has no agenda. It just happens. The Truth is the only thing you'll ever run into that has no agenda. Everything else will have an agenda. Everything. That is why the Truth is so powerful. Give up your agendas and continue to expose yourself, and harmonization will naturally occur.

Los Gatos, California: April 27, 2001

CHAPTER SIX

FREEDOM

The sage Nisargadatta Maharaj was once asked how he became enlightened. He said, "My guru told me that I am the supreme source of all; I am the supreme. I pondered that until I knew that it was true, until I became it." He added, "I was lucky because I trusted what I was told."

Freedom is the realization that this deep, deep peace and this unknown are what you are. Everything else is just an extension of that unknown. Bodies are just an extension of that unknown. The trees outside are just an extension of the unknown in time, in form. Thought and feeling are also extensions of the unknown in time. The whole visible universe, in fact, is just an extension in time of this unknown, this mountain of quiet.

So it's really important to get to the point of maturity where you are willing to look at what is fundamental. There is a difference between pulling the weeds of confusion out and getting to the root of Truth. Did you ever pull weeds from a lawn, grabbing only their tops, and discover they were back again so quickly that it was as if the lawn was never weeded at all? Clearing out identification is like this.

To pull your identification as a limited self out by the root, you must look at it in the most fundamental way. This means you look beyond your usual concern with solving personal problems. Looking at personal issues is like pulling just the top of the weeds out of your lawn: they pop right back up. You may have some relief from the trouble of the day, but the root is still there, totally untouched. But having experiences, even if they clear up problems or offer beautiful insights, is very different than finding the root of who you are. If you don't get to the root, you just get another weed.

And so we ask, "What is the root of this location called 'me'?" You need to know the root of how it began, the genesis of it. There was a moment when that innocent, wordless fascination and love that is your essence moved from being innocently fascinated and in love with *what is* to identification with what is thought. Right in that movement from innocent fascination to identification, that is where freedom is lost. It happened way back in the beginning of time, and it is also happening right now. Each moment there is innocence, the fascination with whatever is, just as it is. But then the mind shows up and says "mine." "That's mine. That's my thought. That's my problem." Or it might also say the opposite, that the thought or problem is "yours." Right at that point lies the genesis, the root, of all suffering and separation.

Being your true self, being your true nature, is different than experiencing it with thought. Realize that you are the mystery, and that you can't really look at the mystery because you are only capable of looking from the mystery. There is a very awake, alive, and loving mystery, and that's what is seeing through your eyes at this moment. That's what is hearing through your ears at this moment. Instead of trying to figure it all out, which is impossible, I suggest you ask, "What's ultimately behind this set of eyes?" Turn around to see what is looking. Encounter pure mystery, which is pure spirit, and wake up to what you are.

The mystery always takes care of itself—as long as we are not addicted to following concepts. This addiction cuts off your access to the mystery. It's like having a jewel in your pocket but you can't get your hand into the pocket to pull it out. When you deeply know that you are the mystery experiencing itself, you realize that's all that is ever happening. Whether you call an experience a me or a you, a good day or a rotten day, beauty or ugliness, compassion or cruelty—it's all still the mystery experiencing itself, extending itself into time and form. That's all that is happening.

If this understanding is held only in your head, you can know it but you are not *being* it. The head is saying, "Oh, I know, I'm the mystery," and yet your body is acting like it didn't get the message. It's saying, "I'm still somebody, and I've got all these anxious thoughts and wants and desires." When we are being it knowingly, the whole being receives the message. And when the whole body receives the message, it's like air going out of a balloon. When all that contradiction, turmoil, and searching for this and that deflates, there is the experience that the body is an extension of the mystery. Then the body can easily be moved by the mystery, by pure spirit.

Imagine that you, as the mystery, step into a body, a different body than the one you have at this time, maybe one that has lots of inner contradictions—one that has lots of opposing wants, desires, and attachments that are at battle with each other. As you sense this "other" body, you can see that the concepts it holds aren't true. Imagine, as you step into this new body, that it doesn't know it's the mystery and so it's really holding on to its identity as a body. Now you, as the mystery, are going to animate and move the body. But since the body believes it needs to be in control, it is fighting you every step of the way. Every time you try to move the arm, there would be tension; every time you opened the mouth, there would be stumbling over words; whenever you as the mystery wanted to experience fascination, you would have to go through all that contradiction and resistance in the body. Even though you had the best intentions in the world and all that energy was flowing through you and into the body, the only way the body could deal with that love would be to turn it into a contradiction. It would become so rigid in response to the energy of this mystery that it could hardly move, walk, talk, or think.

Now just imagine that you hop out of that body and you hop into another one that, on a cellular level, absolutely knows it's the mystery. It looks like a body, and it does everything that bodies do, but it's not really a body; it knows that it's actually just the mystery in form. So when the mystery steps in, it would just be like butter meeting butter. "Ahhh. Okay. Now I can move." And you can just feel what it would be like to be in that kind of body, the one that knows it's the mystery.

In order for that body to be so fully surrendered to its true nature, it would have had to see so deeply and totally that it is the mystery, and to have had all self-image disappear. If it had any remnants of self-image, it would start to stiffen up. As soon as it had any judgment or saw anything as other than itself, there would be stiffness, as if the joints had become rusty. If it was worried about tomorrow, it would just stiffen up. So in order for that body to totally live the mystery knowingly, its personal agenda has to be completely dissolved.

The body-mind cannot dissolve the agenda just because it thinks it's a good idea, but it can happen naturally as beingness sees more and more thoroughly that the only thing that actually exists is itself. It's a visceral thing. Can

you start to get the feel of it? There is nothing to hold on
to. No viewpoints to hold. No separation.

This is why it has always been said that the truth sets
you free. But the *whole being* has to realize the truth. It has
to *be* the truth, knowingly. That's what I mean about the
limitation of picking the weeds and the fruit, replacing
one thought or illusionary belief with another one, a
"better" one. If you put in one self-oriented thought, the
mechanism is going to get contradicted. And if you're trying
to move in that body, it won't move very well. It doesn't
matter which ideas you insert. Some of them may help
you to maneuver a little easier, since some thoughts are
less contradictory than other thoughts and some self-images
are a little less contradictory than other self-images. If you
reframe your self-image to something more positive, the
energy may shift but it doesn't get free of identifications;
it doesn't get to dance. The body becomes free only by
seeing its true nature. This can be done only by going to
the root instead of picking off the tops of the weeds. This
means to wake up and find out what you eternally are
instead of trying to manage your neuroses.

Everything's natural tendency is to self-liberate. That's
the good news. Whatever is held is what keeps total
realization from happening. So when you don't seem to be
self-liberating, you are holding on to something static, ideas
or memories. It could be a big moment twenty years ago,
or it could be a tiny moment yesterday. If you are holding

an identity, an idea, opinion, judgment, blame, victim-hood, guilt, etc., this will get in the way of self-liberation. You can stop holding these stories by *de*-framing, not *re*-framing them.

It's okay to reframe, but it's taboo to deframe. This habit of framing experience by telling yourself a story about it goes very deep, as if putting experience into a better context will help you. It may help in small ways at times, but ultimately it's only when we totally deframe and deconstruct our false views that we wake up from the dream-state of separateness.

The unknown, our own true nature, has the capacity to wake itself up when you start to fall in love with letting go of all the mental structures you hold onto. Contemplate this: there is no such thing as a true belief.

Los Gatos, California: 2001, Date Unknown

CHAPTER SEVEN

THE RADIANT CORE

Winter is an interesting time of year. Many of our most sacred days are in the winter. It is the season of spiritual holidays such as Ramadan, Hanukkah, and Christmas, and often Buddha's enlightenment day is celebrated at this time of year. Winter is a sacred portal, an opportunity. The leaves on the trees are all falling, the fruits drop to the ground, the branches become bare, and everything returns to its most essential root nature. Not only in the exterior world, but also in the interior world there is a natural stripping away.

Winter is also the time of great rains and snow. Every year, the Sierra Mountains become a little less than they were the year before. Part of them is washed down into the streams as the water comes down and returns to its source, flowing into the lakes and the oceans.

Even with its storms, winter is the quietest time of year. There is nothing like the quiet after a storm. If you have had the privilege of being in the mountains right after a snowfall when there's no wind, nothing is moving, the snow is sucking up every sound, and you hear a deep silence everywhere, you know how potent this silence is.

In a real sense, self-inquiry is a spiritually induced form of wintertime. It's not about looking for a right answer so much as stripping away and letting you see what is not necessary, what you can do without, what you are without your leaves. In human beings, we do not call these leaves. We call them ideas, concepts, attachments, and conditioning. All of this forms your identity. Wouldn't it be terrible if the trees outside identified themselves by their leaves? These are very flimsy things to be attached to.

Inquiry is a way of inducing a spiritual winter in its most positive sense, stripping everything to its root, to its core. When we have allowed ourselves to be stripped and really enter into the interior winter, into all the leaves or thoughts falling out of the mind, then we may find ourselves falling backward into, as we say in Zen, who we were before our parents were born. This is a falling into the most essential root of being.

I think there is nothing we, as human beings, resist more than a spiritual winter. If humans did not resist the stripping away of their own identities and allowed themselves to experience wintertime, we would all be enlightened. If we just let wintertime dawn in us, there is a natural stripping away, more like a falling away. When you are very still and quiet, falling away happens naturally.

If you are not trying to control anything, you feel certain thought patterns and energetic qualities falling away like leaves or snow falling; it's a delicate falling. This is what spiritual inquiry is for. Asking "Who am I?" is being present in the space of not-knowing and questioning all your beliefs and assumptions. The realization of eternal truth comes at the expense of all of your illusions.

Of course humans have abilities that trees don't. If trees were like humans, you would see them reaching down with their branches and raking up all the leaves to hold onto them for security. Wouldn't you feel bad if you saw the trees doing this, holding all their leaves to themselves as if they were in an existential crisis? This is our tendency, to pick up the pieces of our pet beliefs and theories, and hold on for dear life.

Sometimes this falling away feels like a powerful storm stripping leaves from a tree. You may have a sacred identity and some wind blows through—usually another human being—and that identity is ripped away. You can be thinking, "I am so enlightened, I can't stand it, it's amazing." Then some wind is going to come along and rip the thought away. Some friend or fellow worker is going to come along and say, "That doesn't look too enlightened to me," and you see it was just another unnecessary identity. If you don't reach down to gather it up, this is a sacred opportunity. Then as it falls you will see that you don't need that identity. It's an illusion, just more dead weight to toss overboard.

Returning to the core, the root of your own self, and seeing through everything that you take yourself to be, allows even your most sacred identities to drop away. There is such beauty in discovering what we can do without. The most beautiful gift of this wintertime is ultimately something that is unspeakable; it is only livable. The winter is actually begging you to just let go, and then let go of letting go. Let this natural and spontaneous returning to the root of your own existence happen. Return to that which is not definable.

There is a wonderful poem about a lone tree with no branches standing at the edge of a cliff in winter, which was written by someone describing his own awakening. A crack opens and runs through the bark of the tree, and then the bark peels off. Imagine cracking a tree or log open to see what is in the core. To see what is inside, you have to crack through to the core. What would you find? You find radiant emptiness, the full radiant emptiness of winter. Imagine something radiant coming out of nowhere, something just radiating out, coming out of nowhere, absolutely nowhere.

When you reach the core that comes after allowing everything to drop, you are naturally cracked open. There is a spiritual heart in that core. You uncover not only the emptiness of the radiant mind, but the radiance and warmth of the spiritual heart as well. When you're really resting, you can actually feel the radiant, empty mind— not as a thought, but as the radiant emptiness of yourself, the no-thingness of yourself and of all selves. You also experience the radiant heart fullness and realize that the emptiness isn't just a bland emptiness—it is heart-full. When the emptiness awakens, you know that it is also the compassionate heart. The warmth of your own spiritual heart comes alive.

Sometimes the winter seems cold, lonely, and isolating. You might find yourself being very still and at rest and feeling very peaceful but wondering, "Where is the juice? Where is the life?" You can be very still and quiet, and even quite empty in a certain way, and still have all the bark intact, without having been cracked open at all. Then you have what could be called the emptiness of emptiness. This is the fully protected form of emptiness.

The true emptiness is when you realize there is much more to it than this protected emptiness. When the bark falls open, when you get to the core, the ideas about yourself and others are seen to be untrue, seen to be just contrivance. You see these as things you were taught and took on, put on like clothes that say, "This is who I am." When the mind is radiantly empty, it's a very alive emptiness. And when the heart is felt to be deeper than emotional, but is not emotionless, not a dead heart, there is sunshine in the middle of winter. Have you ever walked outside on one of those freezing mornings, and it's really cold even though the sun is out, and you think, "How can it be so cold on such a bright, sunny day?" When you are coming from the sun here in yourself, then there is always warmth. The true emptiness is radiantly alive.

Sometimes people ask me, "If I realize that I as a separate identity don't really exist as I thought I did, then who is going to live this life?" Once you touch upon this radiant heart of emptiness, then you know what is living this life, what has always lived it, and what is going to live it from this moment on. You realize that *you* are not living this life; this radiant heart is what is actually living this life— along with this radiant, empty mind. When you give up being who you thought you were and let yourself be who you really are, then this radiant heart lives your life. Then no-thingness becomes your reality, and nondual awareness is what you are.

A great way to think about and explain the true nature of every person (which is all the concept of enlightenment is ever really pointing to) is to say that when true nature is birthed into full consciousness, your mind is open as far as it can go. It doesn't mean your thoughts expand into the cosmos, it means your mind is so open that there are no edges to it. You notice that as soon as you grasp a thought and believe it, the mind closes down onto that thought. So the natural mind is an open mind, and the natural heart is open, come what may. That's the shock of our natural condition—the mind and heart are naturally open and do not know how to close under any conditions at any time. And at the same time, you are beyond even the open mind and heart. Everything is contained within what you are.

The conditioned mind is always taking on God's job, wondering what people are doing and why they do it. But that is none of your business, none of your concern. You can just start walking through life with this natural openness to what is and be that way under all conditions at all times. That's what the true Self has been doing all along. When your true nature is realized, it is not as if you will have some amazing experience, and after that you say, "Okay world, I'm ready." The deepest experience is when you realize that this open, radiant, empty mind and open, radiant heart have always been open. They don't need to open; they are not going to open; openness has always been here. You no longer see two, you see the One in and as everything.

People feel so vulnerable and put up defenses. But putting up defenses is like walking out into the starry night and trying to wrap a little coat around vast infinite space. The vastness just flies out through the arms and the hood. You have this silly little coat out in the vast space and protect yourself inside it and think maybe someday you will open the buttons and be spiritually liberated. Probably not. It's more likely that someday you will stop identifying with the silly little coat. Free yourself of all limiting identities and embrace the infinite.

What allows this opening to take place at a great depth is to realize we are already the openness into which we are opening. If we keep identifying with the human aspect of ourselves, we think, "My God, I am opening into something too big for me." When we really let go and fall into this open silence, we can't find any end to it. It has been eternally here from before the beginning and, in that, our humanness finds a welcoming to open itself. This is so because we are not opening ourselves into a mystery that is alien, or foreign, or different, but into what we have always been.

If you touch the sacred quality of winter inside yourself—that quality of everything returning to its most essential form—you find yourself falling off the end of the mind and into openness. You will start to experience this by not resisting the wintertime and just going with it as it opens you. It can be tremendously revealing, tremendously liberating to just return, return, return. It takes courage to do this. You want to ask, "Who will I be? Will it all be okay?" But just return to the essential. When you find the courage to allow yourself to return to the essential, you are actually returning to the very root of your own self. That's the fullness that the winter has to offer.

It's as if you return all the way to the seed, and only there do you see that the seed contained the whole truth.

When you reach the core of your own being, then you realize that the seed, which seemed very empty when you opened it, is full of the potential of everything that is. Like the seed of a tree, everything that the tree will ever become is contained in that seed. Only in the full return does a full springtime become possible.

These are not ideals I speak about, not goals or potentials. This openness is actually the core of who everybody is. Stop waiting to let go of everything, and then your true nature is realized. When it is realized, then live it. When the living of it happens, life happens spontaneously. Then finally, for once in our lives, we can say with honesty and integrity that it is the most amazing mystery. It is unfathomable. You cannot know it. You can only *be* it, either consciously or unconsciously. But to be it consciously is a whole lot easier than to be it unconsciously. Realize yourself and be free.

Berkeley, California: Date Unknown

CHAPTER EIGHT

SILENCE

The waves of mind
demand so much of Silence.
But She does not talk back
does not give answers nor arguments.
She is the hidden author of every thought
every feeling
every moment.

Silence.

She speaks only one word.
And that word is this very existence.
No name you give Her
touches Her
captures Her.
No understanding
can embrace Her.

Mind throws itself at Silence
demanding to be let in.
But no mind can enter into
Her radiant darkness
Her pure and smiling
nothingness.

The mind hurls itself
into sacred questions.
But Silence remains
unmoved by the tantrums.
She asks only for nothing.

Nothing.

But you won't give it to Her
because it is the last coin
in your pocket.
And you would rather
give her your demands than
your sacred and empty hands.

∾

Everything leaps out in celebration of mystery,
but only nothing enters the sacred source,
the silent substance.

Only nothing gets touched and becomes sacred,
realizes its own divinity,
realizes what it is
without the aid of a single thought.
Silence is my secret.
Not hidden.
Not hidden.

True silence has everything to do with our state of consciousness. I think we're all familiar with what I call a manufactured silence, which is a dead sort of silence. If you have been in meditation groups, you have probably experienced a manufactured silence. It's the kind of silence that comes from the manipulation of mind. That's a false silence because it's manufactured, controlled. Real silence has nothing to do with any kind of control or manipulation of yourself or your experience. So forget about controlling the mind. I'm here to talk about spiritual enlightenment and freedom.

We are surrounded by coarse consciousness. This kind of consciousness is heavy, thick, and dense. When you turn on the TV, you encounter coarse consciousness, for the most part. Most movies you go to have a coarse consciousness. Coarse means asleep within the dream state.

From this coarse state of consciousness, silence is seen to be an object. Quietness is something that seems to happen to you. But that is not real silence. Real silence is your true nature. To say "I am silent" is actually quite ridiculous. When you look at it, it's not that you are *silent*, it's that you are *silence*. Conceptually it may seem to be a small difference between the experiences of "I am silent" and "I am silence," but this is actually the difference between bondage and freedom, heaven and hell.

Stop thinking of silence as a lack of noise—mental noise, emotional noise, or the external noise around you. As long as you see silence as something objective, something that is not you but might come to you like an emotional experience, you are chasing your own projected idea. Looking for silence is like being on a motorboat racing around the lake looking for a smooth spot where everything is silent, and there you are—vroom! vroom!—racing around with increasing anxiety that you are never going to get there. No matter how long you raced around that lake you would never find this silence. Actually, all you have to do is throttle back and turn the key off, and then there you are. Then it is very quiet, very still. When you start to be receptive and allowing, you start to return to your natural state, which is very quiet. Being receptive is just like throttling back. It is a natural state of quiet.

Many years ago I was very lucky to make this wonderful discovery, not because I was intelligent, but out of utter failure. Zen students do a lot of meditating and following the breath. It seems very concentrated, but what often happens is that you think you are following your breath, and then you realize that you are following your mind into some story. It's like trying to discipline a dog that refuses to be trained. Some people seem to be good at that kind of practice. They hold their focus and stay with it and become quiet. I, on the other hand, never had the capacity to hold my mind like that, so I wasn't very good at it. After complete failure time and time again, I heard my teacher say, "You have to find your own way." Instead of closing in on a narrow focus, I found my own way was just to be present, which was to become totally open. This is more like listening than focusing.

In that listening, I discovered a very natural state, a state that is actually the only state that isn't contrived. From that state that is like listening, I started to see that every effort to contrive created another state. As soon as I made an effort, a state would be manufactured out of thin air. I could manufacture beautiful states, terrible states, concentrated states, and all sorts of states; but there was only one state that was totally natural and absolutely effortless. In that state, I found access to the deepest Self, which is freedom.

By its very nature, this state has to be something that is effortless. It has to be something that does not require maintenance. A quiet mind that is arrived at by concentration ends up being a dull mind, not a free mind. It may feel quiet and it may feel good because it's quiet, but it's not a free mind, and in your being you don't feel free either.

This is the kind of peace of mind you get when you have learned to meditate through concentration, and you say to the teacher, "Yes I have found peace, but when I stop meditating it all goes to hell in a handbasket." This tells the teacher exactly what kind of meditation you are doing—you are controlling your experience. When you get up and go about your day and have to pay attention to other things, you cannot pay attention to your concentration, so your peace of mind disappears because it is something that is manufactured.

Half of the practice of spiritual inquiry is to take you to silence instantly. When you inquire "Who am I?" if you are honest, you'll notice that it takes you right back to silence instantly. The brain doesn't have the answer, so all of a sudden there is silence. The question is meant to take you to that state of silence that is not manufactured, where thinking or searching for the right emotional experience fails. If you seek "Who am I?" or ask "What is the truth?" you will notice that these inquiries bring you instantly back to quiet. If you have a resistance to quiet, and most people have a profound resistance to quiet, then as soon as you go back to that quiet state, it is like putting drops of water in a hot frying pan—the mind jumps all over the place looking for something else, for some conceptual answer or image.

The kind of quiet that is natural and spontaneous and not controlled is actually a heartful quiet; it's rich and vast.

Controlled quiet is numb and narrow. When quiet is not controlled, you feel very open, you become receptive, and the mind is not imposing itself. There is a natural return to your true nature. Your true nature isn't quiet; it's quietness. It could also be called no-bodyness or no-thingness. When you come to the true quiet, you have transcended quietness.

As long as you think quiet is in opposition to noise, that's not the true quiet. When you are in the true quiet, you realize that when you hear a jackhammer, that's the quietness—it's just taken some form. True quiet is absolutely inclusive. It goes beyond all dualistic ideas of what quiet is. When we come into stillness, we find that stillness is not separate from motion or movement. After you meditate, if you get up and start to go about your day thinking, "Why can't I keep this amazing stillness?" it's because you've experienced the controlled stillness, not the natural and uncontrolled stillness. As you relax back into true stillness, when your body gets up to move, the stillness itself is moving.

When you allow yourself to return to your true nature, you're not wanting any particular thing to happen in the stillness. Many times when people are quiet, they're waiting for something to happen, which itself keeps them on the periphery, treading water, instead of just letting go. When you aren't waiting for anything to happen, there is a natural sinking and deepening into the source of your own being.

It's very quiet, and then and only then do you start to sense presence. There is a very palpable presence in this quiet. That is why I said this is not a dead quiet. You can sense an aliveness. It's a presence that's inside your body and outside your body. It permeates everywhere. When you are looking for it, you are looking for a gross presence, a heavy presence to hit you over the head. This isn't going to happen. The true quiet is a brightness. You feel bright. There is an awakeness, a deep sense of being alive.

When you become quiet, you let yourself relax into the moment, into your true nature. When this happens, you realize you cannot avoid any part of your experience. If you are looking for quietness to help avoid some feeling, then you are not going to experience the real quietness. The nakedness of quiet or presence disarms you so that you can't avoid any experience, any event, anything. You might avoid things by experiencing a numb kind of quiet, but within the quietness of your true nature, you cannot avoid any part of experience. It is all right here, waiting.

There are many stories or spiritual myths that are created and continue to be perpetuated that portray this coming back to our true nature as a battleground, as if there is something about you that doesn't want to return to itself. Whether it is called the ego, or the me, or the mind that doesn't really want to be quiet, spiritual people can buy into this myth that there is something about them that doesn't want to wake up and that there has to be some struggle. When you are really quiet, you can see that this is total nonsense. You can see that the thought arose in the mind out of emptiness, and only if you accepted it as true could it start a battle. But you see clearly it really isn't true: it's just a spontaneous arising of thought. It won't be true unless you believe it and bring it into the story of the heroic spiritual seeker's struggle. As soon as you involve yourself in the seeker's struggle, you've already lost the war.

You'll see from the silence that every way the mind moves is just a movement of thought that has no reality to it and becomes real only if you believe it. Thoughts are just moving through consciousness. They have no power. Nothing has reality until you reach it, grab it, and somehow impregnate it with the power of belief.

The only way to enter silence is on its own terms. You can't go there with something, only with nothing. You can't be somebody, only nobody. Then entrance is easy. But this nothing is actually the highest price we ever pay. It's our most sacred commodity. We will give our ideas, our beliefs, our heart, our body, our mind, and our soul. The last thing that we'll give is nothing. We hold on to our nothingness because that's our most sacred commodity, and somewhere inside we know this. Only the nothing enters the silence; that's the only thing that gets in. The rest of what we are just bangs at the nonexistent door. As soon as you want something from the silence, you are moved outside of silence again.

Silence reveals itself only to itself. Only when we enter as nothing and stay as nothing, will silence open its secret. Its secret is itself. That's why I say all the words, all the books, all the teachings, and all the teachers can only get you to the door, and perhaps entice you to enter. Once there, you start to feel the presence of silence very powerfully. When this happens, something spontaneously arises that's willing to enter it without being somebody. That is the sacred invitation. Inside you find that silence is the final and ultimate teacher and the final and ultimate teaching. It's the only teacher that won't speak to you. Silence is the only teacher and teaching that keeps our humanness on its knees all the time. With any other teaching or teacher, we find we can get up. We can think, "Oh, I heard Adya said dah-dah-dah, and it sounds good," and we find ourselves lifting up off the floor of surrender. We turn away from our most sacred and beautiful humility.

Silence is the ultimate and best teacher because in silence is the never-ending welcoming to do that which our human heart truly desires, which is to always be with our knees on the floor, always be in that sort of devotion to Truth. Silence is the only teaching and the only teacher that is there all the time. Every minute that you are awake, every minute that you are alive, every minute that you breathe, it's right there.

Palo Alto, California: January 12, 2002

CHAPTER NINE

CONSCIOUSNESS

When consciousness or spirit decides to manifest as an object—a tree, a rock, a squirrel, or a car—it doesn't present much of a problem. However, when it manifests and endeavors to become self-conscious, or self-aware, this seems to be quite a tricky business. I'm talking about human life, when consciousness or spirit is manifest as a human being. In this process, consciousness almost always gets lost. Human beings are by nature self-aware, but it seems that the price paid for consciousness to become self-aware is almost always the loss of true identity.

Consciousness comes into manifestation, which is not a problem, but then it tries to become self-aware. In the process of becoming self-aware, it almost always makes what you could call a mistake. It is not a mistake so much as a blip in the evolution of becoming truly self-conscious. In that blip, consciousness loses itself in what it created and identifies itself with that creation. This blip is called the human condition.

When consciousness forgets itself, it can make all sorts of mistakes. The first mistake that it almost always makes is to identify itself with whatever it created, in this case, a human being. That's like a wave forgetting that it belongs to the ocean. It forgets its source. So instead of being the entire ocean, it suffers under the hideous delusion that it's just a wave on the surface of the ocean. And so it has a very surface experience of itself. Of course, it is still conscious of itself, but it's conscious of something that's incredibly surface and limited. When all it's identified with is a very small wave, it creates all sorts of confusion because that identity isn't true. Anything that's not true quite naturally leads to suffering, and the only reason there is suffering or conflict is ignorance. The identity, at its inception, is a very innocent mistake. It starts out incredibly innocent, but like a lot of things that start out innocent, when it gets farther down the line, the consequences don't seem so innocent.

This is a natural part of the human condition. It seems to be part of the evolutionary development that consciousness is experiencing through a human being. For example, when you think of development as a human, you know that you're born, you go through the child stage and the adolescent stage, and then hopefully if you get out of that, which is questionable, you get to be an adult. You could look back and say, "Well I was really stupid when I was ten years old, and I was even dumber when I was seventeen years old. And then somehow, somewhere between twenty-five and forty-five, I think I got smarter." You could look back and see all those earlier developmental phases as mistakes, as something that shouldn't have been, but that would be a misinterpretation of the facts. It was just a natural part of growing up.

Spiritually, the human condition is a natural part of the evolution of consciousness trying to become conscious through a form. It takes itself to be the form rather than the source of the form. When it makes this misidentification, it suffers under the tremendous illusion of separation. Hence comes the isolation that most human beings feel in their hearts, no matter how many people are around them, no matter how much they're loved. They have to feel alone because they're quite sure that they're different and separate from everybody else.

Fortunately, this is only a blip in the development of consciousness. The human condition, for as many eons as it's been going on, is really just a blip. When somebody wakes up out of that blip, which means consciousness evolves through a human form, it evolves so far that the person matures beyond the blip of separation, much like maturing from a child to an adult. We call that person a liberated human being.

Liberated from what? Consciousness is liberated from the mistake, from false identification and separation. Consciousness, or spirit, is pretty crafty and wise. It has a lot at its disposal as a human being. In life forms with no conscious awareness, the evolution cannot speed up or slow down; it's just going to move at whatever speed it moves. However, when consciousness becomes aware of itself in a human being, it sets up a very interesting dynamic that's not available to any other form of planetary life. The dynamic is that when consciousness wakes up out of the illusion that it's a separate being, consciousness can then use that form to wake itself up in a much larger sense. When it wakes up to the fact that it's really not a wave but it's the ocean of being, it can then use that wave to deliver the message—to get other waves to contemplate this possibility of awakening.

In human beings, this evolution can speed up incredibly because of the conspiracy that consciousness enters into. Once it wakes up in one form, it doesn't have to wait for a natural maturation to happen in all other forms. When that form relates with another form, the awake consciousness relates with sleeping consciousness. Now the sleeping consciousness is much more likely to make this very big leap of awakening. That's the game that consciousness plays in satsang. That's what it's all about.

~

Student: I've been in kind of a rough place since the last retreat. I'm looking at a lot of painful emotions that I've suppressed for many years, and they haven't been pleasant.

I've been witnessing them, learning about them, and burning them up. This is not fun.

Adyashanti: This isn't what you bargained for, is it?

Student: Right. I did what you suggested; I found that part of me that absolutely knows it's fine. And I dove into that trust one-hundred percent. I found a tremendous sense of power and feeling that everything is truly okay, mixed in with these horrible emotions, anger and grief, that are still arising.

But now that I'm in a better place, I've noticed that I'm kind of out of sync. It's like being an awkward teenager, like a boy whose voice is changing—sometimes it's one way and sometimes it's another way. In the past, I didn't need a watch. It didn't matter whether I was early or late, I always arrived at the precise moment for everything to be perfect. And if a situation arose, I always understood instantly why it was arising, and what I should do in that situation, and how it would best benefit everybody there; I could see the whole thing.

But all of that synchronicity is missing now, even though the energy and the positive feelings and the trust are still there. If you've been in a better place and then it deteriorates for a while, it's just so painful because you've seen what it can be like, but you're not there. Is there any advice for somebody who is going through the awkward teenager phase of embodiment?

Adyashanti: The first thing that's important is to have a clear understanding of the context. We can come to a place of deep, profound realization, which is wonderful and very freeing, but the mistake that's often made is that at a later point, when the synchronicity or some other wonderful experience is not happening, we think we have lost something. Actually, that's a particular interpretation that is rarely examined.

What actually happens is similar to the human experience of going through developmental stages. Remember the experience of moving into adolescence, when you're twelve and a half, and you're not there yet, and you're leaving childhood behind? That which in childhood seemed so wonderful is no longer available. The things that had been fun aren't so much fun anymore, but the new ways to enjoy life aren't very obvious. It's awkward and you make mistakes, if they can even be called that. You can look back on that time with a rather clear understanding. It wasn't that you fell away from childhood, it's that you were outgrowing it. As you were outgrowing it, you were leaving it behind. It was uncomfortable because that's how you knew to live life. And yet you still hadn't moved into full adolescence. The same thing happens in moving from adolescent to adult. It can be uncomfortable, but there's no mistake. In retrospect, these are seen to be developmental stages. You outgrew childhood and adolescence rather than falling away from them.

Spiritually, you may come to some very wonderful places, but if they're not complete and absolutely true, then eventually you're going to outgrow them. It doesn't feel good to leave them behind because that's where you're comfortable, and the new hasn't been revealed yet. Then the misinterpretation that's usually made is that you have fallen away from, rather than reached the limitation of, the realization that you had before, as wonderful as it was. When you mature, it's time to leave earlier stages behind. It makes it much harder to leave if you say that you have fallen away from it rather than matured out of it. These are completely different interpretations. With one, you are trying to grasp or get back to what was before. With the other, you look back over your shoulder and bid it goodbye as a nice experience, realizing something more mature is coming.

That's a context I think will help because you see how vital the interpretation you give to your experience is, and you see that the mind is conditioned to give interpretations that usually aren't correct. An incorrect interpretation actually creates more suffering and makes the difficulty many times worse than it needs to be. If you know that, then you'll stop grabbing behind you for what you once had and get more interested in the unknown into which you're moving. You turn all your attention forward. That's really the best thing you can do, nothing other than that.

Student: I think I was doing that, until I came to a place where I was looking at so many negative emotions that I hit some kind of a ceiling. It's very hard to keep looking forward while going through many months of that.

Adyashanti: But that's not looking forward. That's not necessarily what I'm talking about. What happens for most people is that when something negative comes up in their experience, all awareness goes to it like a laser beam. Let's say you're depressed. For most people, all awareness is going to go right there, and suddenly that which was part of a very vast experience of many, many things is now a problem because you've focused on it, and it seems the only significant part of your experience. That's only because the mind has chosen to focus on it and make it the only thing that's happening, even though it is one experience among many.

Student: I see that the negative feelings are a very small aspect of myself, but it's also very clear that I never could see them before. They came up, got analyzed before they were conscious, and then went into some kind of limbo. But they weren't dead. They were just in there, suppressed.

Then consciousness began noticing them before they could get buried. It became a new lesson to be able to recognize these things before they got judged, before they became unconscious. If that's the lesson, how do you allow the difficult feelings to arise but not get caught up in them?

Adyashanti: Well, it's as if we painted black dots on this wall. The dots are maybe an inch round, and three or four inches apart, and the whole wall is covered with black dots. When we walked into the room, the first thing we would usually see is all the dots, right? "My God, this wall has so many dots! It's all dots!" But, in fact, it's not covered with dots. There's a lot more white wall than there are dots. Even if we made those dots really small, the size of a pin, we'd still notice them and think, this wall is full of dots. But there is actually a lot more space than dots. The dots are just where the perception goes.

When awakening starts to arise, all the repressed material starts to arise, and the tendency is for awareness to contract around it. Of course, it seems quite terrible when awareness does this, rather than just resting and seeing everything as a whole. Sure, there's lots of stuff arising, and now that you're aware of it, you can let it arise. That doesn't mean you've got to contract on each thing that comes up. It's much like when you look at the wall with some dots on it and just let your awareness take in the whole wall. Become aware that more of the wall is space than dots. Don't ignore the dots, but don't ignore the background either.

Student: I guess there has to be a trust that if you don't focus on the negative things, they're not going to continue to be repressed. You have to trust that this can be automatic.

Adyashanti: That's right. You would have to enter into collusion to repress them. That's what you've always done.

You pushed them down. But now you're consciously seeing them come up, right? All you've got to do is notice them— "Oh, they're consciously coming up." That means you're not repressing.

Student: I don't have to wait until they melt away. I don't have to watch them melt away. I can notice them and then pay attention to other things—let them do whatever they're going to do.

Adyashanti: That's right. Then it will all reharmonize. But what we usually do when repressed material comes up is to manhandle it, tinker with it, or at least look at it like it's under a microscope.

Student: Make sure you watch it until it goes away.

Adyashanti: Right. Because you assume that it shouldn't be there, you're going to watch it until it goes away so then you can feel safe and relax.

Student: I guess the assumption was that if I didn't watch the negative feelings, they would continue to do what they did before. I definitely know now that that's not the way for me to live ever again. Once I notice them, I can just let them go.

Adyashanti: Yes. It's important to see that repressed material arises from consciousness, and that's where it returns. All of it is impermanent. It's a completely impersonal event—that's the beauty of it. When you know you are consciousness, then there's no repression, and there's no grabbing hold. It's as if you are the sky. You neither push your clouds away, nor grasp them to keep them from leaving you. The sky is inherently completely unaffected, even if the storm comes and lightening cracks and all hell breaks loose. It doesn't much matter as long as the sky remembers that it's sky.

It's very easy to get innocently mistaken. It's like being in a movie theater viewing a movie, and all of a sudden the characters come to life and they invite you in, and so you go into the movie. It seems like everything that happens in that movie has to do with you, and you're very sure you're the movie character. Then for some mysterious reason you wake up and suddenly realize, "Oh, I'm here in the theater with popcorn and a Coke, and all that time I spent thinking I was in the movie was wrong. I'm sitting here watching the movie. I thought it was real, but it's not." This is similar to what consciousness does. It projects this thing called a human being and gets so enamored with its creation that it loses itself in it.

Student: At the place where I'm at, I absolutely know that I'm watching the movie, and I'll be damned if I don't get stuck in it. Suddenly everything around me looks like I'm in the movie. I know I'm sitting in the seat, but all my senses are at odds with that knowledge.

Adyashanti: That's part of the maturing process of learning that your senses, what you think and what you feel, are not indicators of what you are.

Student: Not to be trusted.

Adyashanti: Whatever you may think or feel about yourself has nothing to do with you whatsoever. So you just keep being what you are—which is no-thing. Let your repressed material arise and stay conscious in the process, don't go unconscious or into a trance state. Don't go into analysis either, just allow whatever wants to arise to arise. Question all assumptions all interpretations, all old story lines. Neither repress nor indulge—just be still, inquire, and stay conscious.

Part of not getting caught in illusion is to give up referencing the way we think and feel. A big part of wisdom is to give up referencing the positive thoughts and feelings. We're more than willing to give up the negatives. But when we run into bliss, ecstasy, the joy and release of true revelation, and all the emotions that we consider spiritual, we tell ourselves, "That's me. How do I know that's me? It must be me because I feel very good. I feel bliss and ecstasy and joy. That's how I know who I am, what I am, and that I am safe." But you're still buying into sense perception. If you buy into sense perceptions to tell you who you are, it's just a matter of time until the senses show their other face, which is the negative side, and you'll say, "Oh my gosh, I'm trapped."

Part of the maturation is to realize that you don't just give up the negative perceptions, you give up the positive ones, too. You give up the whole framework that was used to tell you who and what you are. Then, you realize this body-mind experiences whatever it experiences, and you are the conscious space for it to have all those experiences. It truly doesn't matter what the experience is. It just so happens that the more you do this, the body-mind tends to reflect this wisdom by feeling really good. But even when it feels very good and very blissful, you can still fall into the seduction of identifying with those nice emotions. As soon as you get seduced and think that those emotions tell you anything about yourself, it's just a matter of time before you'll be caught in separation again.

The mind wants to land, to fixate, to hold a concept, but the only way you can be really free is by not fixating. That's part of true maturity, and it's one of the hardest things for spiritual people who have had true and profound revelations to go through—to accept the degree of surrender needed to literally let go of *all* experience and *all* self-reference. Even in great revelations, there is almost always something that wants to claim, "I am this." Every time you claim, "I am this," you just claimed another sense perception, thought, emotion, or feeling.

Eventually, when you go through this enough times, the mind gets it on the deepest level and lets go completely. When the mind lets go, you always know who and what you are, even though you can't define or describe it or even think about it. You just know it by being it. This is the ultimate release of identity and separateness.

~

Student: You have been talking about releasing the personal part, but it seems like this is also relevant to meditation. What happens when I meditate is that I get to a place where I'm awake, but I'm not noticing anything, and I immediately say, "What am I not noticing?" Then my mind gets spinning. So this is helpful to me to know that not having any thoughts is the place to dwell in as much as I can.

Adyashanti: You don't even have to try to dwell there because that's actually where you always are already. You may or may not realize that, but right now you are awake. You're just as awake as you are in deep meditation. That awakeness or awareness is just as aware of my voice speaking now as anything else. It's complete, it's whole, and it's never going to be more than it already is. It's already there. This is why all true spiritual teachers have always said that you're already enlightened, you just don't know it.

So the question then becomes, how do I know it? Then you have to start to deeply question all your assumptions about yourself. We have so many assumptions about who we are and what we are, but when we question these, they crumble quite quickly. Then we come into a place where we don't know who we are. And finally, we become very sure that we don't know who we are.

You come to see that every way you define yourself is just a concept and therefore a lie. The mind just stops because it has nowhere to go. The stopping, of course, can't be practiced because any practice stopping is just a fake. This stopping happens as a result of insight, of wisdom, of understanding, and nothing else. It's not a technique. That's why this is the path of wisdom. When the mind understands its own limitation, it stops, and that's very natural. The mind only keeps working to find itself when it suffers under the illusion that it can find itself. When it realizes it can't find itself, it stops because it knows there's nothing for it to do.

When I say the mind stops, I don't necessarily mean that no thought goes through your head. That's not what the mind stopping means. It has stopped interpreting reality. Then you're left with raw reality without any distortion. This is the experience of deep, liberating freedom. It's the relief of a great burden. Your thoughts don't have to stop going through your head. Nothing has to change at all. All your mind has to do is look and get very curious about "What am I really?" The contemplation of the question will lead you right beyond the thought.

If you ask yourself right now, "Who am I?" what's the first thing you know?

Student: First thing I really know? I am the definition I've always given myself.

Adyashanti: Does that mean you don't really know?

Student: Yes.

Adyashanti: So you know that you don't know. Now that's an incredible revelation in and of itself. It's almost always missed because everybody is really sure that they know who they are. You might have walked around five minutes ago without really thinking about it but emotionally being quite sure and acting as if you knew who you really are. It's incredibly significant when a human being can actually inquire and instead of trying to know, tell the truth, which is that she doesn't know. That's a huge truth that is almost always swept under the carpet. When you realize "I don't know who I am," your whole basis for life is suddenly not so firm under your feet.

When you come to the unknown, you haven't made a mistake. You shouldn't try to know because that just takes you into the mind, into an endless loop. True liberation is beyond the mind. So when you get to this unknown, you're actually at the doorway of liberation itself. All you have to do is dive into the fact that you don't know. We live our whole lives quite sure consciously or unconsciously that we do know—and that's our whole experience. What's the experience of *not* knowing? What does it really feel like to not know?

Student: I don't know, but it feels great to think that I don't know.

Adyashanti: Okay, you just answered it. It feels great, doesn't it? If you're not listening to your mind going, "Oh no, I need to know," and panicking, and you go directly to how it feels, it feels very good, very liberating right from the start. It's such a relief not to know because what you thought you were is what caused all the problems. It was the carrier of all your burdens. Now all of that is in question—what if you were wrong? Just the thought is exhilarating, isn't it?

Student: It makes me want to cry, it feels so good.

Adyashanti: Good! So just go right there. Put your attention right there—that's all you have to do. "What's it like not to know? Oh, it's so wonderful." Just let yourself fall into that. You don't come to know by knowing; you come to know by not knowing. Deeper and deeper until you're so deep, you're a million miles away from everything you know, which means you're beyond the mind. Then it'll flash, and you'll know.

Student: I could get trapped in loving not knowing.

Adyashanti: Simply by resting in not knowing, you know. It's a paradox. The more you rest in not knowing, which means never grasping with the mind, the more your direct experience is that you know. It comes in a flash.

Many lifetimes we dance right at the door of freedom. We spin pirouettes on the doormat and never quite know who we are. Just one click, one turn of that knob, and you know—that's all. It's so easy. It's not a matter of it being difficult. It's a matter of people not knowing where to go. As soon as you know where to go and you have the courage to go there, it's easy. Go to the unknown, experience the unknown, be the unknown. All true knowledge awakens within the unknown.

Berkeley, California: March 10, 2001

CHAPTER TEN

DEPTH

Spirituality may be approached in two ways. The first way is the most common, which is through a horizontal movement of the mind. Horizontal movement means the mind goes back and forth collecting information. It's as if the mind comes to a wall that has writing all over it. This wall has all kinds of teachings, practices, things to do, and things not to do. Usually the mind just makes a horizontal movement along the wall, acquiring and accumulating more information. It goes to the left side, and then it goes to the right side, collecting information, beliefs, theories, etc. Have you ever met people whose minds are like that? They have traversed way out to the nether reaches of the wall—the mind spinning horizontally collecting information. That's what the mind does, and most people make this horizontal movement of collecting information, ideas, beliefs, etc., in hopes that it will help them spiritually. But Truth isn't a matter of knowledge, it's a matter of waking up.

We do the same thing emotionally. We move horizontally along the wall collecting experiences. We have basic mundane human experiences, both good and bad, and then as we venture into spirituality we start having spiritual experiences. As with the mind, we start to think, "If I just accumulate enough experiences, then that will mean something. That will get me somewhere." It will get us more experiences, just as when the mind makes horizontal movements, it gets us more knowledge—not freedom, and not Truth.

So the mind, the body, and the emotions play this game called accumulation. They evaluate one piece of conceptual knowledge against another piece of conceptual knowledge. "How does this piece compare to that one? And how does that compare to this?" We like to compare our experiences with others. "What have you experienced? Oh, I haven't experienced that, but I have experienced this; have you?" "This is what I believe; what do you believe?"

Then the emotional body asks, "Is this it? Is this the right experience? Am I having *the* experience? Why don't I have *the* experience?" The body-mind collects more things to do, more techniques, more this, more that.

The mind and body tend to follow old patterns, making horizontal movements, collecting facts, teachings, teachers, beliefs, and experiences. That's the predominant way most people live their lives—horizontally, not vertically. Then they bring that movement into their spiritual lives. But it doesn't matter how much horizontal accumulation of knowledge and experience you have; more information does not equal greater depth.

Now, in this moment, you can realize that you are truly not going to get anything from my words, that whatever your mind absorbs and accumulates as knowledge is not going to get you any more depth. None. Zero. Nothing. It will just get you more horizontal movement. It will just get you more knowledge. Maybe that's what you want, maybe not. But as soon as you realize the limitation of mind, the mind feels very disarmed because it has so much less to do.

There is an invitation beyond the wall of knowledge, which is not to some regressive state before the mind can operate, but a transcendent state that's beyond where the mind can go. That's what spirituality is. It's going where the mind cannot go.

Try imagining you come up to a wall. There happens to be a door in it. You open the door and walk through the wall. Now to get any more depth, you are going to have to leave the wall behind. If you reach back and hold the wall with one of your hands and try to get your feet to walk, you are not going to get very far. So when you really want to get depth, transcendent depth, you are faced with whether or not to let go of the mind. What the mind says is, "I'll let go a little bit, but I'll stuff a lot of that knowledge in my pocket for the journey. I might need my concepts somewhere along the line." It will start to ask lots of questions. "Is this safe? Is this wise? Am I going to be stupid?" As if all wisdom is contained in the collection of knowledge. Mentally, psychologically, people tend to get very insecure when they go completely past their accumulation of knowledge.

The mind can't fathom that there can be a true intelligence, a transcendent intelligence, that isn't the product and outcome of thought and conceptual understanding. It can't fathom that there could be wisdom that's not going to come at you in the form of thoughts, in the form of acquired and accumulated knowledge.

The true spiritual urge or yearning is always an invitation beyond the mind. That's why it's always been said that if you go to God, you go naked or you don't go at all. It's the same for everybody. You go in free of your accumulated knowledge, or you are forever unable to enter. So an intelligent mind realizes its own limitation, and it's a beautiful thing when it does.

When you stop holding on to all of the knowledge, then you start to enter a different state of being. You start to move into a different dimension. You move into a dimension where experience inside gets very quiet. The mind may still be there chatting in the background, or it might not, but consciousness is no longer bothering itself with the mind. You don't need to stop it. Your awareness just goes right past that wall of knowledge and moves into a very quiet state.

In this quietness, you realize that you don't know anything simply because you aren't looking back to the mind for its acquired knowledge. This quietness is a mystery to the mind. It is something unknown. As you go into depth, you literally go into a deeper experience of what seems to be a great mystery. Now the mind might come in and want to know what's going on and start to define everything, but that's not going to bring any more depth. The mystery just keeps opening to itself if you let it—if you let go of control.

As acquired knowledge is left behind, what is found is that you have left your familiar sense of self behind. That self only existed in the accumulation of knowledge and experience. Something very interesting happens when you leave it all behind, because you are literally leaving your memory behind. You leave behind who you thought you were, whoever you thought your parents were, and everything else you thought and believed. Yesterday is gone. Then a very interesting thing starts to be noticed: you can leave all of that behind and still you *are*—you are right here and right now. So what you are becomes even more mysterious.

When you realize that you can leave every self-definition behind and still you *are*, then you begin to see that these thoughts must not be what you are. In other words, who are you when you are not thinking yourself into existence? Who are you when you give up all thoughts, even the ones that you are not supposed to question, such as, "I am a human being. I am a woman or I am a man. I am somebody's daughter or son." You start to see that when you are not thinking yourself into existence, who you have taken yourself to be literally isn't there anymore. If this "you" can disappear like that and reappear as soon as you think it into existence, how real is it?

In that moment of recognition, you have already begun to move beyond the wall of accumulated knowledge. Then, if you don't redefine this moment or rebox it in some concept, rethinking yourself into existence, your true state of being starts to present itself. What you really are begins to awaken. The true *I am* is so unbelievably empty. It's so free of everything you thought you were. It has no limitation. It has no definition. Any definition would be a disservice to what you are. All that's left is consciousness, and it's not even that because that's just a word.

When you see what you really are, no concepts apply anymore. You are so empty there is just consciousness. There is no inner child, and there is no adult either. None of your identities exist until you think them into existence. Consciousness can look down and see there is a body, but that's not the source of anyone's problem. The problem is what you add on after that in your mind.

In this emptiness you start to taste the experience of *being*. This is *being* before you are something or somebody. And this mystery of being is what's awake and alive. It is the only thing that doesn't need the mind to conjure it into existence. You don't have to think at all to be this awakeness. Everything about you changes except this one fact of consciousness. The body changes. The mind changes. Thoughts change—much more quickly than most people would like them to. And no matter how much knowledge you acquire, that knowledge is not going to get you *here* any faster. *Being* is the one constant—*that* which is always awake.

Now the mind, if you go back to its knowledge, has all sorts of ideas about what your true nature must be because you have read about it so much, have heard spiritual teachers talk about it, and there is a whole mystical mythology created around Truth. Of course it's quite a shock to realize that's not it. Whatever you think you are, that's not it. Even if your concept is very spiritual, mystical, and other worldly, you are not that concept.

Letting go of accumulated knowledge helps the identity shift from the me-self to the no-self Self. When this happens, it is called spiritual awakening. But this doesn't mean you can't use your knowledge. Knowledge is still there when you need it. You can dip back into it to tell you how to operate your computer, and for all sorts of other useful things. Nothing's been lost except your false identity. You don't become an idiot. You don't forget how to tie your shoelaces because you realize you weren't who you thought you were. But the mind is afraid of this. The biggest barrier to realization is your thoughts about it because thoughts will create images of the awakened state, and those images just belong to accumulated knowledge. No matter what image you have of your true Self, that image cannot be the Truth. When you see this, it becomes easy to experientially recognize what's right here. Just what's right *here*—eternal consciousness, pure spirit.

Once you realize this deeply, not with the mind or through deductive logic, but through a direct awakening, then everything else becomes rather simple. Once your world of conceptual knowledge gets put in its rightful place, it is transcended. You see that you are eternal consciousness now appearing as woman or man, this or that character. But like every good actor, you know you are not what you are appearing as. Everything that exists is consciousness appearing as, or God appearing as, or Self appearing as, or spirit appearing as. The Buddha called it no-self. When that's seen, you see Unity. There is only God. That's all there is: God appearing as a floor, as a human being, as a wall, as a chair.

No knowledge, no statement of the Truth touches what's eternal, what you really are. And no statement about how to get there is true either, because what gets one person there doesn't get another person there. A mind that likes to look for the one true path cannot find it. Of course, the mind doesn't like that. "No right path? Nothing that could be said or read that ultimately, in the end, could be true? The most enlightened being can't speak the Truth?"

No. It's never been done, and it never will be done. The only thing you can do is to put a pointer on the wall that says, "Look that way." A false spiritual arrow is one that points *to* the wall and says, "Look *this* way." A true arrow is one that points beyond the wall of concepts.

The pointers can be more or less true, but no matter what the pointer says, no matter how it says to get there, it doesn't say anything about what's beyond. Nothing. Because as soon as you are beyond, as soon as you are being what you are, nothing applies anymore. That's why so many of the great spiritual teachers have said that there is nothing to know. In order to be free, in order to be enlightened, there is absolutely nothing to know, and there is no enlightenment as long as you think you know something. As soon as you absolutely know that you don't know anything and there is absolutely nothing to know, that state is called enlightenment because all there is is *being*. When there is Oneness, *who* is the One going to know about? The One knows only, "I am that. I am this." As it says in the Bible: "I AM THAT I AM." This is true awakened knowledge. All other knowledge is secondary.

Knowledge that is used for a given means or a given purpose is strictly utilitarian. When you start to see this, you stop looking for the Truth in anything you know. Instead, you look for the Truth in what you *are* because, when you find out what you are, you find out what everything else is, too. It's all One. You see that there is nothing to know, and your focus of inquiry shifts from thought to *being*.

Everybody has had transcendent wisdom break through into the mind. When you've wracked your brain with a problem for a long time and then, for some reason, you've stopped struggling, and then all of a sudden you got an "Aha! That's it," where does that come from? Wisdom has broken through. It could be something really small, a day-to-day kind of thing. It might register in the mind as an "Aha!" but it isn't a product of thought. It came from somewhere else, from *being*. So *being* has great wisdom. It's a shock because we are not used to operating from that wisdom, which seems to break through only every now and then. But actually your beingness is operating that way all the time.

Lots of things are relatively true, but nothing that arises from the mind is absolutely true. What a relief it is for the mind when it no longer has to struggle, and your whole orientation, spiritually speaking, moves from knowing to being.

Palo Alto, California: March 28, 2001

CHAPTER ELEVEN

EGO

The fall guy of spirituality is the ego. Since there is really no one to blame for everything that happens in our lives, we manufacture this idea called the ego to take the blame. This causes a great deal of confusion because the ego doesn't really exist. It is simply an idea, a label for a movement to which we have attached our sense of self.

When we consider that the ego is just an idea that doesn't really exist, we can see that many spiritual people are blaming it unfairly for all the things they believe they should get rid of. They misunderstand that something arising inside of them—perhaps a thought, feeling, predisposition, or moment of suffering—is proof of an ego, thinking that just because it arose, ego exists. They think they have an ego because of all these things that point to it. All we ever find is this proof or evidence that ego exists, but we can never find the thing itself.

When I ask someone to look for the ego, he or she cannot really find it. It isn't there. An angry thought or emotion triggers the belief, "Oh, I've got to get rid of that—that's my ego." It's as if everything that's happening in a human being, especially a human being who is interested in being spiritual, gets used as proof of the existence of an ego that must be annihilated. And yet nobody can find it. I have yet to have somebody show me the ego. I've seen lots of thoughts, feelings, and emotions. I've watched expressions of anger, joy, depression, and bliss, but I have yet to have one person present me with the ego.

Many people present me with an assumption that because all these things exist, there must be a fall guy, somebody or something in themselves to blame. That's the common understanding about ego. But that is not ego. Things are sometimes as simple as they appear. Sometimes a thought is just a thought, a feeling only a feeling, and an action just an action, with no ego in it. Now the ego that exists, if there is any ego at all, is the thought that ego is there. But there is no evidence whatsoever for this ego's existence. Everything is just arising spontaneously, and if there is any ego at all, it is just this particular movement of mind that says, "It's mine."

Now usually this thought, "It's mine," follows the arising of a thought or emotion. It might be, "I feel confusion— it's mine," or "I feel jealous—it's mine," or in response to whatever other experience is arising, "It belongs to me." One thinks there was ego present, and it caused this thought or feeling or confusion. Yet every time we go directly back to find the ego, we find that it was not there prior to thought but followed afterward. It's an interpretation of an event, of a given thought or emotion. It is the after-the-fact assumption that "it's mine." Ego is also the after-the-fact interpretation that says, "It's not mine," the rejection of a thought or feeling. It is easy to see that such a position implies that there is somebody there whom it doesn't belong to. That's the world of duality. It's my thought, my confusion, or whatever it is, or it's not my thought, not my confusion, not mine. Both of these are movements or interpretations of *what is*. Ego is only this interpretation, this movement of mind, and that is why nobody can find it. It's like a ghost. It's just a particularly conditioned movement of mind.

From early childhood, we are given messages such as, "You are pretty," "You are smart," "You got a good grade, so you are good," or "You did not get good grades, so you are not good." Soon the child starts to believe it, to feel it, to own that emotional essence as "me." In the same way, someone can have a thought, and pretty soon he or she will start feeling that thought. If he thinks about a happy, sunny day, soon his body will start taking on that tone, feeling something that doesn't exist. So of course this makes it rather difficult when someone is told to get rid of ego, because who is going to get rid of ego? What is trying to get rid of ego? That's how it maintains itself, thinking it has to do something with itself.

Ego is a movement. It's a verb. It is not something static. It's the after-the-fact movement of mind that's always becoming. In other words, egos are always on the path. They are on the psychology path, the spiritual path, the path to get more money or a better car. That sense of "me" is always becoming, always moving, always achieving. Or else it is doing the opposite—moving backward, rejecting, denying. So in order for this verb to keep going, there has to be movement. We have to be going forward or backward, toward or away from. We have to have somebody to blame, and usually it's ourselves. We've got to be getting somewhere because otherwise we are not becoming. So the verb—let's call it "egoing"—is not operating if we are not becoming. As soon as a verb stops, it's not a verb anymore. As soon as you stop running, there is no such thing as running—it's gone; nothing is happening. This ego sense has to keep moving because, as soon as it stops, it disappears, just like when your feet stop, running disappears.

When we really let it in and start to see that there is no ego, only egoing, then we start to see ego for what it really is. This produces a natural stopping of a pursuit toward or a running away from something. This stopping needs to happen gently and very naturally because, if we are trying to stop, then that is movement again. As long as we try to do what we think is the right spiritual thing by getting rid of ego, we perpetuate it. Seeing that this is more of the same egoing will allow stopping without trying.

You could find a hundred oak trees and each would have a personality but no ego. So the stopping of this verb called ego has nothing to do with the personality stopping. It has nothing to do with anything we could put a finger on: not a thought, not a feeling, and not ego. If we had to stop or the world had to stop in order for us to be free, we would be in big trouble. It is the movement of becoming, the moving toward something or away from something, that stops.

A different dimension of being starts opening up when this verb ego is allowed to run down. Just by watching, we can start to see that nothing that arises has an egoic or "me" nature. A thought arising is just a thought arising. If a feeling arises, it has no "me" nature and no self nature. If confusion arises, there is no "me" nature in the arising. Just by watching, we see that everything arises spontaneously, and nothing has an inherent nature of "me" in it. Egoic nature comes only in the afterthought.

As soon as that afterthought is believed, then we have a whole world view happening—"I'm angry; I'm confused; I'm anxious; I'm so happy; I'm depressed; I'm unenlightened" or, worse yet, "I'm enlightened." Suddenly this I-thought belief colors everything we see, everything we do, and every single experience that happens. People think that spirituality is an altered state, but this delusion is the altered state. Spirituality is about waking up, not about states.

My teacher once told me, "If you wait for the mind to stop, you're going to wait forever." I suddenly had to rethink my avenue to enlightenment. I'd been trying to stop my mind for a very long time, and I knew I had to find another course of action.

The spiritual instruction to "just stop" is not directed to the mind or to feelings or to the personality. It's directed to the afterthought that takes credit and blame and says, "It's mine." Stop! That's where the teaching of stop is aimed. Just stop that. And then, in that moment, feel how completely disarmed the sense of me feels. When the sense of me is disarmed, it doesn't know what to do, whether to go forward or backward, right or left. That's the kind of stopping that's important. The rest is just a game. Then, in that stopping, a different state of being, an undivided state, starts to emerge. Why? Because we are no longer at odds with ourselves.

The mind may hear these words and ask, "What is an undivided state of being?" That is to miss what is happening right now. One *feels* an undivided state of being; it cannot be found in some abstract and conceptual realm because that realm is itself a divided state. We touch the undivided state when we allow ourselves to be disarmed, when we're not trying to prove or deny anything, and we stay in that sense of being disarmed without resistance. A state arises of literally being in the body and beyond the body, and the body is no longer at war with itself. The mind may or may not be thinking thoughts, but those thoughts are not at war with each other. Become curious about the true nature of yourself, about what you really are, because that curiosity opens you up to the undivided state. From the undivided state, one of the first things realized is that you don't know what you are. Before that, when you knew what you were, you were divided—endlessly. From here, where there is no division, there is not the heavy, restricted, confined sense of self. You become a mystery.

Division makes it easy to find a sense of self. If we are angry, for example, that's where it is. But when it is just anger and there is no identification with it, even anger all of a sudden unfolds itself. It's an energy that arises and dissipates by itself. And then what am I? If it's not "my" anger, if "I'm" not the divided one—what am I?

Allow the mystery of *being* to unfold in a way that is experiential. Start on the level of being rather than thinking. As the mystery unfolds, we get brighter and brighter just being this present awareness. And then the sense of identity begins to shift away from defining itself through division and internal conflict. The mind finds there is no hook on which to hang an identity, so identity starts to deconstruct itself in openness. Mysteriously and paradoxically, the more identity deconstructs itself, the more alive and present we feel. The sense of self becomes like sugar dissolving into water until it's as if there isn't a self, and yet we still exist. Buddha might have said, "All the sugar dissolved—there is no self." Ramana Maharshi might have said, "The sugar dissolved into the water, so the water and sugar are the same thing—there is only the Self."

The ultimate freedom from the nonexistent ego is to see that it is actually irrelevant. As long as it is perceived as relevant, it keeps "becoming." All of the good intentions in the world just fuel it. "I'm getting rid of myself more and more every day, and someday I'll be completely rid of myself and have absolutely no ego." What does that sound like to you? It's the ego. But when the me is seen in a moment of insight to be irrelevant, the game is over. It's like someone who is playing monopoly and thinks his life depends on winning the game, when all of a sudden it dawns on him that it is irrelevant—it doesn't matter. He might keep playing. He might go get a sandwich. This life is not about winning the spiritual game; it's about waking up from the game.

There is still this other part in us called "conditioning." This is not ego. Conditioning is conditioning; it's not ego-conditioning. Conditioning is like installing a program in the mental computer. When the program is installed, it doesn't mean the computer has an ego. It's just been temporarily conditioned. By the time we get to be adults, the body-mind has been fully conditioned. That conditioning has been blamed on ego, but conditioning didn't come from ego. Ego is the afterthought that arises in the wake of conditioning, which is where all the real violence happens.

When it is seen, that conditioning is like programming provided by genetic coding, society, parents, teachers, gurus, etc. (the mind also starts to condition *itself*, but that's another story), then we begin to recognize that conditioning is without any self. The mind is afraid to see that because, if the conditioning is without any self, there is no one to blame. There is no use blaming ourselves or anyone else any more than we would blame our computer when we put a disk in it. Look in the present moment to see what conditioning is there, and it will be seen that there is no blame in it. It's part of existence. Without conditioning or programming in our bodies, we would stop breathing, the brain would become mush, and there would be no intelligence—that's conditioning, too.

What keeps conditioning firmly anchored within us is that we interpret it as "mine." Then, of course, there is blame of oneself and others, and there is trying to get rid of the conditioning because we believe "I created it," "I didn't create it," or "I can't get rid of it," and the mind doesn't like that. The mind is deluded in thinking that it can get rid of this conditioning but, when truth gets in, one becomes less and less divided. When conditioning arises, if it is not claimed as "mine," it arises within an undivided state. This could also be called an unconditioned state of being. When conditioning meets an undivided state, there is an alchemical transformation. There is a sacred miracle.

When something arises, one can have the experience that "this is me" or that "I'm back here—that is not me." Both of these are movements of mind, of afterthought, which is better known as ego. But when the undivided state occurs, two things may happen. The first can be an awakening to our true nature, which is this undivided state, this undivided being. The second thing that can happen is that the conditioning, the confusion that was innocently passed on through ignorance, can reunify itself. When conditioning arises within a person who is in an undivided state, where he or she neither takes ownership nor denies it, then there can be a sacred alchemical process through which the conditioning reunifies itself all by itself. Like mud in water, the conditioning naturally just sinks. It's like a natural miracle.

This can be very delicate because, if there is the slightest ownership or the slightest denial of ownership, that process is in some way corrupted. It asks of us an inward softness and openness because this undivided sense is very soft, and we can't search for it like a sledgehammer looking for a nail. That's the reason spiritual teachings stress humility, which helps us to enter the truth of our being in a gentle and humble way. We cannot storm the gates of heaven. Instead we must allow ourselves to become more and more disarmed. Then the pure consciousness of *being* becomes brighter and brighter, and we realize who we are. This brightness is what we are.

When it gets very bright, we see that we are this brightness, this radiance, and then we start to realize from our own experience what this human birth is all about. This brightness comes back for itself, for every bit of confusion, for every bit of its suffering. Everything that the me tried to get away from, the sacred Self will come back for. This bright Self starts to discover its true nature and wants to liberate all of itself, to enjoy itself, and to truly love itself in all of its flavors. The truly sacred is the love of what *is*, not a love of what could be. This love liberates what is.

The true heart of all human beings is the lover of what is. That's why we cannot escape any part of ourselves. This is not because we are a disaster, but because we are conscious and we are coming back for all of ourselves in this birth. No matter how confused we are, we will come back for every part of ourselves that has been left out of the game. This is the birth of real compassion and love. For too long it has been said by spiritual traditions that you have to slay so much to get to love. But that is a myth. The truth is that it is love that really liberates.

Santa Cruz, California: May 27, 2001

CHAPTER TWELVE

LOVE

Everyone is acquainted with the kind of love that is celebrated in songs, poems, commercials, and high school romances. This kind of love is beautiful, but I want to speak about love in its essence, in its most profound sense. Love is an important aspect of Truth. Without love, there is no Truth. Without Truth, there is no love.

Anyone who has been lucky enough to experience very deep and embodied love knows that love transcends all experiences and emotions. If you have experienced this love, you know that it is present even when you are not in the feeling state called love. If it is not real love, as soon as you fall out of the feeling state, you realize the feeling is all you had; it's like a car that just ran out of gas. That's not the real love, the deepest love, the foundation of love. When you really love, you know that love transcends all experiences. For example, a mother loves her child even when the child is driving her up the wall. She knows that even in difficult times when she is upset, there is still love.

If you have ever loved a friend, you know there is love even when you don't feel it, even when it is a difficult time. The deepest, deepest caring transcends all experiences.

Of course there are many different expressions of love. But when you point to any experience of true love, you know love exists even in the absence of that experience. Every time you name it, or say "This is how love is" or "This is how love feels," you notice that it also exists in the absence of that definition. You can't really get your hands around it and say "This is what true love really is," because it transcends that. It's kind of like a self. It can't be found. So you might say, "I can't find a self so there must not be one." And yet, there is something that is awake and shining and conscious, even if that something is radiant nothingness.

In the same way, the love aspect of Truth is always present when Truth is present. This love transcends the ebb and flow of emotion; it is a love that is always open. If you extract your openness, then love is dead, Truth is dead. This love is something that causes us to be deeply connected in some unspoken way, and it happens when we are really available, really open. Words neither amplify nor take away from it. When we turn our attention to that which is unspoken, there it is. There is the connection—something beautiful, something intimate happening. When we are open in this unspoken way, we feel as though openness meets openness.

All of you have experienced a time when you knew this, and for whatever reason you severed that openness for some other agenda. Something came up and you went "snip!" and that connection was gone; then the lie was spoken. When you disconnect from this unspoken level, it's as if you have said, "I'm just about to start lying, telling what's untrue." It's easy to lie when you cut off the heart of love. If you stay connected at the heart, it is very difficult to lie or to tell a half-truth. If you refuse to disconnect from love, then every relationship you have will be totally transformed; even the relationship with yourself.

It may seem a little strange to hear this because you were once taught that the connection of love is to be reserved for special moments, with special people, in special circumstances. It's taboo to have this connection be indiscriminate. You may have thought, "I'll save it for you, and you, and you—but the rest of you are pretty scary." But this that is awake, this love that transcends all description, when it is known as a deep connection and deep unity, this love is indiscriminate. It doesn't know how to turn itself on and off. That switch is only in the mind. This love is always on. It loves saints and sinners equally. That's real love. Imitation love is, "I love you more than I love anyone else because you fit into my little twisted world view better than anyone else does."

True love is synonymous with Truth. It's not different than Truth. It's not the love of going to the prom with the perfect person. That's fine, of course, but this is something different. The deepest essence of love doesn't fall in and out. Love is, period. It loves even people your personality might not like. This is not because we develop it or become holy, noble, or saintly. That has nothing to do with the love I'm speaking about. This love is a deep and simple recognition, something intuitively knowing and meeting itself in each experience, in each being, and in each pair of eyes. It meets itself in everything that happens. It's the love simply for the fact that there's anything happening at all, because that's the real miracle. It could so easily be that nothing exists, much easier to have nothing than something. It's a miracle that anything happens and we live in this abundance called life.

This depth of love isn't something that we fall into or out of. The love that we fall in and out of is somewhat removed from the essence of love. That type of love is also part of life experience for most human beings, but this love is just recognized to *be*. It is a great surprise the first time we recognize it—when we find that this love, right here, coming directly from ourselves, is in love with whatever it meets.

"How can this be so? I'm not supposed to love that person who has a different philosophy than mine."

"What is that love doing here? We are at totally opposite ends of the political spectrum."

"Why do I love you? How did that creep in? What kind of love is that?"

This is a deep love. This is a love that's synonymous with Truth. Where this love is present, Truth is present. Where Truth is present, this connectedness, this deep love, is present.

Many of the stories of Jesus describe this kind of love. People around him were constantly telling him what wasn't lovable: "This prostitute, we'll stone her to death. God doesn't love people like that." But Jesus, totally connected, knew this love is indiscriminate. It doesn't come because someone is nice or noble. It just is. It loves everyone indiscriminately. Most of his ministry was founded upon this kind of love. It was even expressed for those who were responsible for his death. He said, "Father, forgive them, for they know not what they do." That comes from the love that just will not stop, even in the face of death. That is the voice of love. The mind may say, "Hey, they are going to kill me. I have a right to withhold love." But the truth doesn't operate by that law; it doesn't play by the rules of the game that the mind would make up. It loves anyway. Make no mistake: this love doesn't have anything to do with you becoming noble, holy, and worthy. This is a love that's pre-existing. It has always been here and always will be here. It's a love that simply is.

You had to discount this love to get on with the business of being a separate self, but still it existed. And this is actually our greatest fear, to find out that you love all sorts of things and people that your mind would rather not love. Possibly the only fear greater than death is love, real love. Finding out that you do love, that this is your nature, is the beginning of the end for everything in you that thinks it is separate. When you get upset with people, it's really because the love is there and you don't want it to be. That's why people who get divorced are often at each other's throats. They think that since they are getting divorced, there shouldn't be love. But it is there. You may not like it, you may not want to live with someone, but the love is still there because there is no such thing as loving once and then not loving. When people are able to face the fact that the romantic part of love may be gone but the caring or connection is still there, it can actually free their energy. And you might as well get used to it with one person because you will find eventually that it is there with all beings. It's just there. It's a done deal. It doesn't matter who it is. If you can accept love you will know when to stay with someone and when to leave them.

True love has nothing to do with liking someone, agreeing with him or her, or being compatible. It is a love of unity, a love of seeing God wearing all the masks and recognizing itself in them all. Without it, Truth becomes an abstraction that is sort of cool and analytical, and that is not the real Truth. The Truth exposes itself in the willingness to open to this intimate connectedness with everything. Whether the personality likes it or not, an intimate connection is there. Sometimes it will rush to the fore and make itself known in a very obvious way. Sometimes it will burn in the background like embers, just there for everything. With this love, you can feel the walls of opposition come down naturally in the acknowledgement of a deep connection. Not only do the walls of opposition fall, but love is felt for every human being and for life itself.

It is like the love of a parent for a child: even though you feel frustrated at times, this love is constant. It is similar to life, which might drive you bananas at times or be really nice. This love is beyond the good moments and the difficult moments, which continue to happen. When you have awakened to this love that transcends every good and bad moment, a radical revolution occurs in your relationship with life itself. This is a love that has no opposite, such as hate, but is present through everything, in all moments. When you realize this, it is a revolution because, when you see that this love that you are loves the unlovable, loves what you're not supposed to love or what you were not allowed to love culturally, and is not paying attention to the separating rules of ego, you realize this is a different kind of love.

Please understand that this love of which I speak is not exclusive in that it does not exclude other experiences of love. Friendship love, marriage love, and many other kinds of love have their own way of being and moving through the world. But I'm talking about the essence itself, the essence that is within all the flavors of love. This is the real spiritual love, which is a deep unspoken connectedness. Only this love has the power to transform our relationship to being alive, our relationship with each other, and our relationship with the world. This love is timeless. This love is uncontained.

Many times when people are awakening to this love, they will tell me, "Adya, it's just too much for me—its going to tear me apart." Ridiculous! Too much for you? You're transparent. You are empty. It just goes through you and beyond. Through you and beyond! It's only when you hold yourself in a particular way that it feels like too much. You are holding an idea of your personal boundary, your edge, and of course you can't contain it. Love was never meant to be contained.

Berkeley, California: September 2002

CHAPTER THIRTEEN

SPIRITUAL ADDICTION

A spiritual person can become addicted to spiritual highs and miss the experience of Truth. Spiritual addiction occurs when something great happens and it feels as if you have received a hit of a great drug. As soon as you have it, you want more. There is no drug more potent than spiritual experience. The intellectual component of this addiction is the belief that if you just had enough of these experiences, you would feel great all the time. It's like morphine. You get a hit of it in the hospital because you break your arm, and you think, "If I had a little drip going all the time, life would be relatively pleasant no matter what happens." Spiritual experiences often become like this, and the mind puts them into its familiar pattern, thinking, "If I had this experience all the time, that would be freedom."

Soon you find that your condition is not much better than that of a common drunk, except that drunks know they have a problem because it's not culturally acceptable to be a drunk. The spiritual person is very certain that there is no problem, that his or her inebriation is unlike the other forms of inebriation, and the whole point is to be spiritually inebriated forever. That's the mindset of an addict: "I got it and I lost it. I need it. I don't have it."

In our culture, with most kinds of addiction, the addict is understood to be miserable. But not in the spiritual world. The seeker is told that spiritual addiction is different from all the other addictions. You're not a junkie. You're a spiritual seeker.

This problem will last as long as there is something in you that holds out some hope for the high experience. When that begins to break down, you start to see that pleasant, wonderful, and uplifting experiences are some-what like very pleasant and uplifting alcohol binges. They feel great for a short time, and then there is an equal and opposite reaction. The spiritual high is followed by a spiritual low. I have seen this in many students.

Once these high and low experiences have played themselves out for a long enough period of time, it starts to dawn on you that maybe the high spiritual experience is just a pendulum swing followed by a low experience. At some point, you may have an ordinary moment and get on to the fact that these pendulum swings are equal and opposite reactions. You realize it's impossible to sustain one part of the pendulum swing because its nature is to move back and forth. There's no way you are going to pin that pendulum to any one point.

This is the movement of the seeker, but it's also the movement of the me because the me is always interested in opposite and equal reactions, trying to sustain one experience and avoid other experiences. That's what the me does. It chases after the good and avoids the bad. As long as identity is in this movement, even if it's at the spiritual high point that seems very noble, you are never going to be free. There is no freedom in this because there is no such thing as sustaining an experience. By its very nature, freedom doesn't have anything to do with sustaining a particular experience because the nature of experience is to move. Like a clock ticking, it continually moves.

We have to discuss this issue of spiritual addiction because, unless you understand it, the second point I am going to make will just be another fancy spiritual concept. But if you get the first part—that spiritual awakening is not about any particular high experience—then the second part becomes much more meaningful and interesting. The second part is that everything is consciousness. Everything is God. Everything is One. Seeing that everything is One shoots a hole in trying to pin the pendulum swing of experience in any particular place. If it's all One, it's no more One when the pendulum is in the high state than when the pendulum is over in some other state.

Zen teachers don't explain anything in an abstract way, which is both the beauty and the terror of it. My teacher's way of explaining this would be to hold up his staff and say, "This is Buddha." Then he would bang it on the ground, and everyone would think, "Wow! That's really wild Zen stuff. I wish I knew what he was talking about." Then he would go—bang, bang, bang, bang—and he would say, "This is Zen. This is it!" And everybody would react, "Oh wow!" People would wonder, "What? Where?" but nobody would say that. "It couldn't be *that* because that's just beating a stick on the ground." Since it's not all One to the mind, the mind keeps looking for it, "Where is it? What state is it?" Because the me references everything to its own emotional state, that's what it uses to decide what is true. It thinks that what is true is always a spiritually high emotional state, but this stick pounding is not a very spiritually high emotional state. Then, to make it worse, to make it more horrifying, he would say, "This is a concrete description of the truth. This is Buddha. This is not abstract." Then we would really be defeated.

It is a real blessing to have a teaching that insists upon being concrete because he could have just said, as I sometimes do, "Everything is consciousness. It's all One." Then the mind thinks, "I got it. I'll buy that. I know what that means." But when a stick bangs on the ground and the teacher says, "That's it!" you can't wrap your mind around it. That banging of the stick is as much God as you're ever going to get. Everything else after that is an abstraction, a movement away from the fact. In Zen, no concessions are made to abstraction. This is both Zen's power and its curse because it forces students to realize the real thing instead of thinking they understand something when they don't.

This puts a spiritual seeker into a dilemma. In contemplating what it means that everything is One, the me starts looking for an experience of Oneness. Then it reads a book about the experience of Oneness, and sees a description of merging and losing oneself in the tree bark or somewhere else, and starts hunting in past emotional experiences to find if it's had that kind of experience.

The merging experience is very pleasant and very beautiful, and you may or may not ever have it. If you have a particular type of body-mind, you might experience having it every five minutes. If you are another type of body-mind, you might have it every five lifetimes. It means nothing whether or not this happens or how often. I have met many people who can merge at the drop of a hat, and they are about as free as a dog chasing its tail in a cage. Merging has nothing to do with being free or actually having any idea what Oneness really is. Oneness simply means that everything is the One. Everything is That, and everything always was That. When there is a very deep knowing that everything is One, then the movement of the me trying to find a past experience ceases. Movement is cut off. Seeking is cut off. The seeker is cut off. Realization cuts everything off all at once. Every experience that you will ever have is the One, whether that experience is merging or having to go to the bathroom. Even when it's beating a stick on the floor and saying, "This is it. This is the Buddha. This is enlightened mind. It doesn't get more enlightened than this!" It is all God.

This realization often starts to dawn when the me, who thought the experience of Oneness was related to the pendulum swinging to a high emotional state, begins to see how limiting that belief is. The experience of "I've got it and I lost it" is a very, very valuable experience for the spiritual seeker. The beauty of the swing of experience is that it starts to force the me to let go of any conceptual framework about the experience itself. You question the delusion that the experiential quality of any moment tells you anything about the ultimate nature of reality. The personal me thinks that when it feels good, it is closer to its true nature, and when it feels bad, it is far away from it. But after living in this I-got-it-I-lost-it swing, eventually that me stops believing its own delusion. Something starts to see through it, recognizing that this isn't freedom.

Now if the seeker is programmed to do so, the seeker will hear what I'm saying and think, "Forget it. I still believe that I can pin the pendulum swing up to a high spiritual state and stay there." The entire existence and identity of a spiritual seeker can be invested in this pendulum experience. It is disorienting to realize that you spent your life, and perhaps many lifetimes, trying to pin your experience on a high emotional state, and all it has led to is becoming a spiritual-experience junkie. This can bring you to a new low and a great disorientation. If you feel this intense disorientation, you may try to move away from it because all of a sudden the seeker in you doesn't know what to do. It gets very confused and wonders, "If I'm not chasing the high to be free, what am I doing?"

The seeker needs to stay right in the middle of that disorientation and that sense of not knowing what to do because, by staying there, without resistance and without moving away from it, in that moment something new starts to be born. Feel in your own experience what starts to be born when you let yourself experience the disorientation of the spiritual seeker who stops seeking a different experience than the one that is happening right now. You can feel the seeker dissolving and the peace emerging, which is the peace the seeker was always looking for anyway. As the seeker dissolves, then the peace is born, and there is stillness. This is not a quality of stillness that has any dependence on an emotional state. At the moment when the seeker starts to dissolve and there is just peace, then the pendulum might swing into a high spiritual state or into a very ordinary state, or even into an unpleasant state, and the peace itself remains completely independent of those states. This is the dawning of the realization that only from the place where the seeker is dissolving can freedom happen because there is no longer any movement toward or away from experience.

The nature of experience is that it changes or undulates like the waves on the ocean. It's supposed to be doing that. Identity starts to shift from "me," the seeker, chasing some particular experience, to just this. Just this. The center is always right here. The center always was right here. It's just the seeker that insisted the center could be in the spiritual high experience. But as the seeker dissolves, then right here is where every instant is the center. It's motionless right here. And you can be having a very ordinary, a very unhappy, or a very extraordinary emotional and psychological experience, and still the center is right here. And only from here does it begin to dawn that everything is an expression of the center. Everything. There is no expression that is more the truth than any other expression. There is no experience that is more the truth than any other experience because, in the center of it all, there is no seeker. Right here, there is nothing. All is One.

You will discover there is no little "me" in the center occupying the space. Without this me in the center, there is nobody to judge whether a given experience is the right experience or whether it is spiritual. Do you get it? This is it! When my teacher banged his stick on the ground, he showed that everything was arising out of the center where nothing is. All is an expression of that center, and is not separate from that center. If you don't see it *here*, you're not going to see it anywhere. This is the Great Release— the release from having to change anything to get to the

Promised Land or to search for the enlightened experience. The enlightened experience is that nothing needs to change. In fact, you can see from here that enlightenment itself is not an experience. And it's not a spiritual high.

So every experience is just an expression of that which is not an experience. Everything is that, and there is nothing but that, and there never was anything but that. This is what it really means to know that everything is One. That's why all the sages throughout time have said, "This is the Promised Land." This Oneness is God. This is the One. This is *it*. It's not somewhere else. And as soon as the center is seen to be empty, and you know there is nobody there looking for it to be other than it actually is, this is much better than the highest of the high spiritual states. As nice as those are, the Truth is infinitely more free.

∽

Student: Would you explain the distinction between spiritual experiences and moments of nondual awakening? It seems possible to get hooked into trying to recreate what was actually a temporary nondual awakening.

Adyashanti: All I am saying is an experience is an experience is an experience. Now it is true that one could glimpse the nondual state. What usually happens is that if the seeker has not been seen through, the seeker will very quickly reassert itself and will link the nondual state with its byproduct. The byproduct of the nondual, nonexperiential state of seeing that there is nothing to seek, there never was anything to seek, and that everything is God is a big "Aha!"

The mistake that the seeker can make, if it hasn't been thoroughly seen through, is to associate the "Aha!" with the nondual, nonexperiential state. Of course the "Aha!" can just be relief, happiness, laughter, tears, or bliss, all of which are byproducts, which are very beautiful. It's not to say that what was seen wasn't the Truth. It's just to say that unless the seeker has been seen through thoroughly, the seeker will start once again to associate those experiential byproducts with the awakening itself. The byproduct will become the goal. It does become the goal.

So I'm not saying that what was seen was untrue or that nothing of value happened because the byproduct is very beautiful. I'm saying, can you start to clear away all the byproduct? Can we see what is the *source* of the byproduct?

Student: Along those same lines, would you agree that you offer a sort of deconstructionist technique of becoming more free, where we see through the misconceptions that bind us, then work to disentangle them? It seems to me that the kind of openings that we are talking about can also happen through other techniques like meditation. If we work on constantly embracing these openings, then through repeated experiencing, they become sort of ingrained in the body-mind system, and there is a flowering that happens at some point.

Adyashanti: Well, it's possible that it works that way. It usually doesn't. Usually the seeker has particular experiences, but then doesn't have them, or has them with a relative frequency, whether it's once a week, once a month, or once a year. From what I've seen, the myth that is propagated is that if you just keep having those experiences, something is going to change. Sometimes something does change. Most of the time the seeker goes right along having those experiences at a relatively predictable interval. You can almost chart it. They believe that these will eventually pay off at the end of the line. The seeker believes that they are moving toward enlightenment. That's a myth.

What I'm saying is, most of the time it just doesn't work that way. I'm not saying that it can't. I'm just saying, most of the time it doesn't work because the seeker is thinking that the next experience, which is going to be different from this one, will be the right one. That's the illusion that usually goes unquestioned, and if it's unquestioned and uninvestigated, then one can continue to have spiritual experiences, even with great frequency, and it's like getting loaded all the time. You just drink more often, right? You can have spiritual experiences with great frequency, but it doesn't mean you're not still an addict. The seeker is firmly in place.

Student: This raises for me a question about trusting our experience. If you eat something that disagrees with you, you don't eat it any more. You try to avoid it, and that's called wisdom or being smart. And if something works for you and gives you an experience of freedom, there's a God-given natural feedback loop that says, "Go in this direction." So how would you advise dealing with the natural tendency to associate a particular action with the spiritual experience or opening that came with it? Are you saying that we shouldn't follow that feedback?

Adyashanti: No. I'm saying just the opposite. I'm saying you actually should follow the feedback. You should follow your experience. The only problem is, most people follow part of their experience, and they don't follow all of their experience. Part of their experience would be to believe, "If I do this, then I will get an experience of freedom, and that's very nice, and that's what it's all about." Or, "From my own experience, I know that if I do this, at some point Grace strikes and I will get this nice experience." I'm not arguing with that at all. That's part of one's experience. Another part of one's experience, which is often not looked at, is the fact that this progression, this movement, is itself bondage. It is not freedom. It is always waiting for the next experience. People's experience shows them this; they know that this is so. They know they are not really free because they are waiting for freedom. And this waiting is also their experience, but usually it's almost instantly discounted because that part of the experience threatens one's entire spiritual paradigm. So the seeker doesn't look at that.

Student: Yes. I don't want to look at that.

Adyashanti: I am saying to trust your experience, but trust the whole of your experience.

Student: It sounded like you were challenging the idea that evolution happens. You know, there are stages. There are steps. You do go from point A to point B. There must be some place to go, otherwise we wouldn't be here talking about something to be done. Isn't there a progression?

Adyashanti: There is a progression, but you're not going anywhere. If anything, it's a regression more than a progression. When it's valuable—and I don't mean regressing into an infantile state, not that kind of regression—you regress from all of your spiritual ideas into a much more simple state. In that sense, there is certainly a regression that can happen, and the point of it is that one does come upon what I'm talking about. It can come about suddenly, all at once, and it can also come about gradually, much like butter melting. Now if we want to call butter melting a progression, I suppose we could, but I think saying that butter melts is something other than a progression. You're not getting anywhere. You're actually getting nowhere fast. So it can happen either way. It can happen in a gradual or a sudden way. It has been my experience with many people that it can happen any way it wants. So in that sense I can buy into the progressive theory, but not into the idea that some experiences tell me that I am making more progress than other experiences.

That's the catch. They don't indicate you are making any more progress.

Student: That's the part I feel is a little dangerous because I think that we all want some measuring stick of having made progress, and we tell stories about it here in satsang.

Adyashanti: We do.

Student: We talk about how this predicament happened to me last week, and I feel I handled it better—like satsang is working. We have a sense of improving and that life is getting better.

Adyashanti: Yes, of course there is improvement, but improvement is not awakening or enlightenment.

Student: Obviously, there are all kinds of experiences. We can be fooled by them. And I really hear what you're saying: Don't get hung up on the glitter. Go for the fort. Don't capture any silver mines or gold mines and get hung up in them.

Adyashanti: Right, because they'll all run out. If your experience is that your life is getting better and better, or more and more free, who am I to argue with that? That's your experience. If someone is having that experience, then I'm really glad they are going to be happier, and they are probably going to treat themselves and others much more kindly. That's fine. As far as freedom goes, there is really no gauge to it. You're either awake or you're not.

Palo Alto, California: January 31, 2001

CHAPTER FOURTEEN

ILLUSION

The world is illusory.
Brahman alone is real.
The world is Brahman.

~ Ramana Maharshi

The world is Brahman, the ultimate reality if perceived directly. But this world has an overlay, which is made up of the demands we make on the world. Everybody has his or her own demands. Some people feel like the world hasn't given them enough. Some people believe the world is not safe enough. Some people demand that everybody be peaceful. The various demands one can make on the world or on oneself go on and on. These demands form an overlay. When it's said that "The world is illusion," that means this overlay doesn't exist. It is not real. It is only a function of the mind.

When someone tells you, "I love you" and then you feel, "Oh, I must be worthy after all," that's an illusion.

That's not true. Or someone says, "I hate you," and you think, "Oh, God, I knew it, I'm not very worthy," that's not true either. Neither one of these thoughts hold any intrinsic reality. They are an overlay. When someone says, "I love you," he is telling you about himself, not you. When someone says, "I hate you," she is telling you about herself, not you.

World views are self views—literally. This world of perceptual overlay is not actually happening except in the mind. A good way to get a picture of this is to imagine you are dying. Everything that dies with you is all that wasn't real: your whole view of yourself, your view of the world, the way it should be, the way it could be, the way you should be, the way you could be, whether you were enlightened or unenlightened. All of these ideas are gone once the brain stops ticking away. It's not actually here. None of it is actually happening. That's why spiritual awakening has an element of death.

If you really want to be free, you've got to be prepared to lose your world—your whole world. If you're trying to prove your world view is right, you might as well pack your bags, and go home. If you want to wake up and find, "Hallelujah! I was right about it all," just go on vacation or back to work, and don't drive yourself crazy on spiritual matters. But if it's slightly appealing to think about waking up and realizing, "Oh, I was totally wrong. I was totally wrong about myself and about everybody else. I was totally wrong about the world," you might be in the right place.

People can be sitting in meditation to prove their world view is right without knowing it. This can be for both negative and positive reasons. One person might be thinking, "I know I'm a Buddha. I know I'm enlightened. I know I'm enlightened." But even with that thought you are trying to force a world view, and it never quite fits. The Zen Master Huang Po encouraged people to throw away the Buddha—to throw away all views, all the world views, even the spiritual world view—so you are not imposing it on what is. That's where the phrase, "If you meet the Buddha on the road, kill him," comes from. If you have any image of what the Truth is, slay it immediately because that's not it.

Releasing this overlay of ideas and images is very much like awakening from a dream. Waking up is the only way to realize it is a dream. We can be very fundamentalist— even with Eastern teachings, you know. You can believe there is no world or there is no self, but if it's not something that is directly experienced, then it's another form of fundamentalism. It's another way the mind imposes something upon what is.

When you sit in meditation, you begin to recognize the various points of view you have carried, and you can let them go. But as fast as you let them go, you'll replace them. It's like belief. Most people don't let go of one belief without grabbing another belief. This one is better, so I'll take this one now. But to question the one who is holding the beliefs is much more efficient than to question each little belief along the way, because you will see through one but soon another one will pop up. It's kind of like pulling weeds.

My best friend across the street when I was a little kid had a back yard with a lawn that was actually more weeds than lawn. His father would pay us twenty-five cents an hour—mind you, that was thirty years ago—to pull up the weeds. But even then we knew twenty-five cents an hour wasn't a lot of money. But an hour of work would get us a candy bar. At first we would sit in the yard digging up the weeds with little dinner knives. Well, that was too hard, so then we just started pulling the weeds. We would pull the tops off the weeds. There were more weeds than lawn, and so we would pick, pick, pick for hours a day and for up to two weeks at a time in the summer when we decided we really wanted money. By the time we got to the other end of the lawn a week later, the first weeds we pulled were already coming back up. This is how beliefs are. You pick one, but if you don't get to the root of it, if you don't pull out the one who holds the belief, new beliefs keep appearing to grab your attention. This is a good way to guarantee yourself a job. The ego can stay in business that way.

So uprooting the one who is holding the beliefs is what it is all about. Who is the one who is holding this belief? Who is the one who is struggling? Who is the one who is not struggling? Once you uproot the one who is holding the structure together, then the whole structure collapses. If I pull the root out, then the whole conceptual structure collapses. If you leave a piece of the root, it's going to come back and start building again.

~

Student: Sometimes I see my world views as illusions, and I feel wholeness. But then I become caught up again in separateness. What does it take to stop moving back and forth, to move from occasional moments of realization to constant realization?

Adyashanti: Dissolve the one who asks, "When will it go from moments of realization to constant realization?" Do you have a sense of the one who is asking that? It's a particular movement of thought that is asking.

It's all just a conceptual overlay. There is a saying in Zen: "One minute you are a Buddha, the next minute a sentient being." Sometimes you are Buddha. Sometimes a sentient being. And it's always Buddha because both are masks. Sentient being is a mask. Buddha is a mask, too. When the masks are dropped, both the sentient being and the Buddha are the same.

Student: And you can't call it anything.

self-reflection

Adyashanti: You can't call it anything. It is no-mask, emptiness. As Huang Po said, "It is not greater to be manifested as Buddha and no less to be manifested as sentient being."

Student: I notice a tendency in me to be attached to this feeling of free fall.

Adyashanti: To be attached to feelings of free fall is still to be attached. And it's the cause of suffering because there won't always be pleasurable feelings. Feelings will change. In the seeing of it, there is the letting go of it. There is a spontaneous relaxation of the holding on to even wonderful experiences. We go beyond realization, beyond ego mask, and beyond Buddha mask. In pulling away the dense mask in front of emptiness and going beyond—there is just the great "Ahhhhh."

∽

Student 2: When you talk about having no concepts or illusions and realizing emptiness, that seems to be a place beyond love. In my experience, that love also arises in this awakening, and it seems to be like an energetic field between illusion and emptiness. Will you talk about love and how it fits into awakening? How is it that with so much love inside of us we humans so seldom feel loved?

Adyashanti: The first movement of emptiness is love. That's also the first calling, which is the same thing, the same love. It leads to this whole universe, the creativity of this existence, and the birthing of it. It's just like a mother. All arises out of that indescribable sense of love and beauty. It is the first expression of nothingness. In that sense, love is often a portal or doorway into the truest, deepest state. I think the reason that human beings don't feel love is because they are disconnected from themselves, which *is* love, the source of love.

This whole human mechanism is just love incarnate, creativity incarnate. The ego can't see this. It finds itself incapable of allowing that kind of love in. Only our true nature can allow it in without being overwhelmed by it. That's why often in spiritual communities the teacher is not simply loved, but worshipped, because an ego can't take that much love. People might even feel this love in themselves, but since it feels like too much to the ego, the love is projected onto the teacher.

We tend to project our own Truth, our own beauty, somewhere else. We project our own beauty. That's the unconscious deal that's made. "I, somehow, through decision or ignorance, decide to be a separate somebody. But since I'm not actually a separate somebody, I've got to give away my Truth. But since I can't get rid of the Truth—it's not going to just disappear from the universe—I've got to put it somewhere else. If I'm going to pretend to be this limited somebody, I've got to give away my divinity to somebody else." Then it goes to Jesus or the Buddha or the spiritual teacher. "Somebody has to hold it while I'm busy being me." That's the projection.

I think that when there is love, in its truest sense, we are actually falling in love with our own Self. We are falling in love with what our ego can't hold. When we get past the business of being a separate somebody, we are going to take back our true nature and take ownership of our Self so that we can actually look at the Buddha—or the sacred figure or our own teacher—and know directly and absolutely, "This is me. It's the same." We can only do that when we have actually taken that richness totally back to ourselves and seen it as our own Self.

Then there is a great love and appreciation. That's what I have for my teacher. It's more like, "Thanks for holding my projection. Thanks for holding my enlightenment while I was busy pretending not to be enlightened. Thanks for not holding on to it or owning it, but for giving it back. There is just so much love and gratitude here for that. Thanks for showing it to me."

There is a saying in Zen, "When the realization is deep, your whole being is dancing." You can have an experience of emptiness, but it can be the emptiness of emptiness. A phrase that's used is "a cool emptiness." But when it's the true emptiness, your being is dancing. It even goes right through your physical body. Everything is alive again. You are dancing—the emptiness is dancing. Then we go deeper into that love and that dance and that joy. Then it settles, and it is still love, dance, and joy, but it settles into something that is quiet and very pervasive. There is a love and a stillness that's just deepening.

When awakening happens, the heart has to open. I think that for realization to be complete it has to really hit on three levels—head, heart, and gut—because you can have a very clear, enlightened mind, which you'll know in a deep way, but your being won't be dancing. Then, when the heart starts to open just like the mind, your being starts to dance. Then everything comes alive. And when your gut opens up, there is that deep, deep, unfathomable stability where that opening, who is you, just died into transparency. It's become the absolute. You are That.

There is an expression, "solid emptiness." In the mind, the emptiness isn't so solid. It's very space-like, ethereal, and that's enlightenment on the level of mind. Enlightenment on the level of heart is an aliveness, a sense that all of me is dancing. The enlightenment on the level of gut is an emptiness that is similar to that of the mind, but it's like a mountain, a transparent mountain. All of these are expressions in the human being of the Truth.

Student 2: That is the most beautiful thing I've ever heard. I have wondered about spiritual groups that have bypassed love and do not seem to operate from there. They don't have that center and seem very dry. I've always wondered how there can be awakening without that.

Adyashanti: As my teacher used to say, "It's so easy for spirituality to become just talk." There can be a certain level of enlightenment of mind, of total clarity—an awakening as space or spaciousness—that can go on and on. But even with that, there can be, and there very often are, very subtle forms of the individual *me* protecting itself. As soon as you drop below the level of the neck, self-protection becomes an immense issue for many people. It's one thing to change my mind or have no mind or be nothing, but when that starts to come into the heart, it is getting really close to home. That opening is of another order of intimacy. And so I think some spiritual communities can miss it because some people can be very enlightened in their mind but nowhere else.

Student 2: What strikes me is that's why I was drawn to you. With some spiritual teachers there can be many experiences and a lot of exercises for going into altered states or *samadhi* states. But what you really add that not a lot of teachers do is the full embodiment of the beingness here. That's where the love has to come in. If your spiritual life is only about going into altered states, you don't have a lived beingness, and you don't think you need it. You're deluded by the idea that that's all there is or that's enough.

Adyashanti: As the awakening descends, you come into whole different areas of your being that are going to be seen through. When you get down below the neck, you get down and dirty, if you know what I mean. It's like the spiritual time to put on your gloves, and there is a lot of human seeing on a very deep emotional level that's required to really get there. If we are stuck, as you say, the spiritual state may actually be used to protect us from having to die more completely. So the high spiritual states are some of the most effective hideouts because they can seem so blissful and so complete. And there you are having these amazing experiences, but you are still kicking your dog when you come home from work.

Different spiritual traditions seem to embody different aspects of realization. Zen embodies the level of gut. That's what it aims at. In Zen, dropping really deep into that is called The Great Death because there is a total letting go of everything, even the attachment to the heart. In the same way we can be attached to the intellectual enlightenment, we can also be attached to the heartfelt enlightenment, which is why in Zen you hear so much talk of void. This is the mountain of emptiness, which is the substance, actually, of existence.

Boulder Creek, California: October 25, 2001

CHAPTER FIFTEEN

CONTROL

What if you let go of every bit of control and every urge that you have, right down to the most infinitesimal urge to control anything, anywhere, including anything that may be happening with you at this moment? Imagine that you were able to completely and absolutely give up control on every level. If you were able to give up control absolutely, totally, and completely, then you would be a spiritually free being.

Many people have said that when you dig down to the deepest, deepest level of human emotional makeup, the primary emotion that keeps human beings separated is fear. I haven't found that to be true. I find that the core issue that keeps human beings experiencing themselves as separate is the desire and will to control. Fear arises when you think you have no control. Or you become afraid when you realize you have no control but haven't yet given up the desire for control.

When I am talking about control, I am talking about everything. The most obvious kind of control occurs when human beings are trying to control each other. If you think back to any particular conversation you had today, chances are you will find in it some element of trying to control. You were trying to control someone's mind so they would understand you, agree with you, listen to you, or like you. This may not be true for all conversations and people, but probably is for quite a few.

I am talking about everything from the most obvious forms of control and power to the more subtle forms of control. In these, we try to change our experience of right now. One of the most common questions I get goes something like this: "Adya, I've had some sort of spiritual awakening thing happen, at least I think I have, and even though it has happened, I don't feel like it is totally complete. I don't really feel like I'm totally free. I may actually have awakened to what I am and who I am, and that's been very beautiful and profound but, Adya, something hasn't totally completed itself." What follows is, "What do I do?" I have yet to see a single case of someone who is in that predicament who isn't dealing primarily with the issue of control. Not one, because everyone is dealing with the condition of control unless they are totally liberated from the desire for control.

In a very simplistic way, the difference between those people who have had deep and profound spiritual awakenings to their true nature and those who are actually liberated and free is this very simple matter: those who are liberated and free have totally and absolutely let go of control. This is true because, if you let go of control, then you cannot help but be liberated and free. It's like jumping off a building. You can't help but go down; gravity pulls you that way. If you totally let go of control, you end up in complete self-realization.

In its most elementary form, the desire for control feels as if there is a clenched hand in your gut. What you find, when you have worked your way through all the various ways you would control experience, is this elemental closed fist. And when you get close to this closed fist, you will find it has a protector. The protector of our elemental sense of control is rage. Usually this rage is more destructive than any feeling you ever wanted to admit could possibly exist within you. It is the ultimate protector of control because, if you have ever been near somebody who is raging, you get away from them, unless you're stupid. You might be drawn to lots of other things: somebody whose trip is victimhood or depression, or maybe someone who's a victimizer or has other patterns. People can be drawn into an attachment or enmeshment with all sorts of emotional patterns, but very few are actually really comfortable with or find much value in being drawn like a moth to the fire of rage. In that sense, it's a very good protector. It does its job very effectively.

Many people never get to their rage because right above it is fear. Fear usually works. Most people who are terribly afraid will run away. But the few people who go through their fear will come out of it feeling like there is something seemingly tremendously destructive underneath. And if you can keep going through that tornado, you will find there is an existential grip, usually in the pit of the gut, which can survive even very profound spiritual awakenings. The fear may or may not survive, and the rage may or may not survive. Often they don't. But the grip sometimes does survive in its most elemental form.

That's why I suggested that you imagine what it would be like if you were totally without any movement of control within you, any desire to control, any ideas to control— whether on a very obvious level or on the most profound level of your own experience. Imagine what it would be like for the desire to control to be completely absent from your system.

This desire to control is, ultimately, our unwillingness to be fully awake. There is a wonderful little story told by Anthony DeMello. He was a spiritually awakened Jesuit priest who lectured and wrote books and who died in the 1980s. He tells the story of a mother knocking on the door of her son's room saying, "Johnny, you've got to wake up. It's time to go to school."

Johnny answers, "I don't want to wake up." Mom repeats, "Johnny, you've got to wake up!"

"I am awake!"

"Johnny, you've got to get up, and get out of bed, and go to school!"

"I don't want to get out of bed."

Does this sound familiar? "I don't want to go to school. I'm tired of school. Why should I have to go to school?" She answers him, "I'll give you three reasons why you have to go to school. Number one, because it's time to go to school. Number two, because there is a whole school full of students depending on you. And number three, because you're forty years old and you're the headmaster."

This is similar to many human beings who have had a very deep awakening. It's like the alarm clock went off, you've stopped dreaming your illusionary self into constant existence, and you know that you are ultimately pure spirit. You have experienced that. You're like the headmaster lying in bed when it's time to go to school. You're awake, but you haven't totally agreed to be awake. You haven't given up your control. You want to stay in bed, but everything is calling you out. Life is calling you out, and the last bit of control you've got left is just to say, "No. It's scary out there. I don't know if I want to go out that door. That's a whole new life out there. That's a whole different way of being. I've awakened, but I'm not sure I really want to be completely awake. I thought I was just going to be able to awaken and then still stay in this bed."

It's funny that when people actually get to this particular place in their spiritual evolution, when they have had some deep awakening and yet they are really dealing with the essential issue of control, they often ask, "Do you think I should go to someplace like a monastery? I wish I could just go on retreat forever, and do you think that's a good idea?" And I always say no. It's like that schoolmaster saying, "Wouldn't it be the best thing to just sit in bed for the next twenty years?" Is that going to solve your problem? Absolutely not! You've got to get up and get out. And you are going to have to let go of control to do it.

This is a very profound and very deep movement. It's really a mutation at the very core of your inner self. It's not necessarily a revelation, a spiritual attainment, or a realization. It is a fundamental mutation in the way that we exist—to live free of the will to control. When you come to the core of control, most likely you will feel like you're going to die. Most people do, because in a certain sense, you *are* going to die. To have life become suddenly and totally not about control, even at the most fundamental level, is a death. For most of us, our whole life became about control by the time we were about a year old. You can see children even at two years old trying to control their mother, ordering and manipulating mommy and daddy. It starts so young, this urge to control, this sort of biological sense that I'm going to survive if I can control.

This is really a fundamental transformation. That's why I say that we can have a very deep and profound realization of the truth and, in the end, the final real freedom doesn't necessarily come about through a realization. It comes about through a deep surrender at the deepest seat of our being. Of course, most people are going to need a profound realization of their true nature in order to be able to surrender naturally and spontaneously. But it completes itself with a blind and unpredictable release of control. Of course the thing that people ask me about this point is, "Now, how do I do that?" And all I can say is that question itself is your control. Control is trying to do its thing. The question of how is always about control. It may even be useful at times to have a how, but ultimately it's about control. There is no how. Just let go.

∼

Student: What do you mean by unpredictable?

Adyashanti: By that I mean, in the final giving up of control, the will to control, everything is unpredictable. It's the last thing we want to face because everything is totally unpredictable. In other words, everything is completely unknown.

Student: And so the unpredictable letting go of control happens simply by being in the unknown—and at that point is the opening. Is that right?

Adyashanti: You can be there and still not let go. If we are really resting somewhat in our true nature, the obvious forms of control aren't functioning. If they are, then we are not resting in our true nature. We are nowhere near it. If we are obviously trying to control ourselves and others, we are totally back in dreamland. But even if we are resting very deeply, it is possible, and in my experience with people, even probable, that this existential grip of control is still there. It may not even be noticed at that moment, but it is there in potential.

Student: There is fear with this.

Adyashanti: That's the fear of the death. Yes. Because the letting go is through experiencing the death of our separate self, and that is a very deep, profound death. Very deep. Of course, it's a totally illusionary death.

Student: Does letting go happen when we die?

Adyashanti: No, not at all. You can have physical death and still maintain a desire for control right through two hundred thousand lifetimes.

Student: So is letting go of the existential grip a physical thing?

Adyashanti: The existential grip is felt physically, but it's much deeper than physical. As an example, imagine that you had an absolutely convincing experience that you, as you think of yourself currently, were going to totally survive when your body died. This wouldn't be a belief, it wouldn't be hope, it wouldn't be faith—you just knew one hundred percent. Would you be very afraid of your body falling away and dying?

Student: No.

Adyashanti: I think most human beings are not really afraid of their physical death because, if they had the conviction that *they* don't die, they wouldn't care about their body dying. What they are afraid of in dying is not that "my body dies," but that "I die."

Student: Me as I know myself.

Adyashanti: Yes, "I" die. And if I didn't think I would die, I wouldn't care if my body died. But the fact is that the one who is afraid of death is the one who is holding on. The me I know myself as, my personality, is toast. It's gone. But it's an entirely illusionary death because the me is just a collection of familiar thoughts. But if I am identified with it, it doesn't feel like an illusionary death at all, does it?

Student: So, would it then happen over time?

Adyashanti: It happens when time runs out. It *can* happen over time. It can be very sudden or it can also be very gradual. There is only one rule: there aren't any rules about how one unfolds.

Student: Should we just stop asking questions?

Adyashanti: No, that will not work either. That's too much control.

Student: But when you start asking questions, you are trying to control something.

Adyashanti: Yes. But if you stop yourself from asking questions, you are trying to control, too. The best thing that human beings can do for themselves is to always be absolutely, totally, and completely coming from an honesty with themselves, a total internal integrity. If there is a question that's very important, deep, and very real for you, ask it. Do you see what I mean? It's more important to hold with the integrity of what is within you than to sell it out for an idea. That holding of integrity is what takes people completely into truth. Not many people will do this. They are all measuring what is inside of them with a concept coming from the outside. If you take what I said tonight to mean that all questions are forms of control, which is true, and therefore you stop asking questions, that would be a rotten thing to do because then you would just be controlling in the opposite direction.

Student: Does the questioning part ultimately cease?

Adyashanti: Yes. That's the whole point. The questioning part ceases when the questioner ceases. Everything the questioner asks is a means of tightening the grip.

Student: To defend itself?

Adyashanti: Right. Even when this grip is asking for release and for surrender, it's still trying to control. It's saying, "I want surrender now." So one's own deepest integrity is the most important thing. My teacher used to say something that was very simple, but very profound, "Only the phonies don't get enlightened."

Student: You mean they don't want to know the truth?

Adyashanti: I don't know if they don't want to know the truth, I just know that most people find it very difficult to hold real integrity with themselves over a sustained period of time. They keep giving it up for all sorts of reasons, ideas, and concepts. They are following the teachings of four hundred books simultaneously, doing anything to avoid what is actually going on inside. As soon as they look inside and come from their own deepest integrity, then everything starts to open up. They may have a ton of questions. They may suddenly have no questions. It doesn't matter. They are coming from their heart, and they haven't sacrificed it for anything or anybody. That's where everything is powerful.

If you look at the human beings throughout history who are seen as exemplars of very spiritually awakened people, there is one thing you can always find at their central core: They are always people who had an absolutely ruthless honesty and integrity with themselves. It's rather rigorous for a human being to do that because we usually run into our own insecurities, fears, and doubts.

Student: Does that imply that it's hard to do it in your daily life?

Adyashanti: No. It's rigorous, but daily life is really no impediment. People have gone off to temples, monasteries, and ashrams for millennia. If you look at all the people who have done that, how many people actually get enlightened? The success rate is pretty rotten. Even today, you can ask someone, "How long did you live in the ashram in Japan or China or Tibet or India?"

"I was there for fifteen years." Well, you know the bottom line question if we are talking about spirituality, not just religion: "Did you get it? Did you get what you went for? I remember you said that you were going there fifteen years ago to become enlightened. Has it happened?"

That's the bottom line, isn't it? When you clear all the other stuff off, you either did or you didn't, and when you ask most people if they have found enlightenment, the answer is, "No." I'm not saying it's not useful for some people to go to monasteries because clearly it can be. What I am saying is that right where we happen to be, wherever that may be, whatever we happen to be doing, when we begin to let go of this will to control, we realize that there is really no better place to be. Our excuses run out.

Have you ever had your excuses run out in anything in your life? When your excuses run out, all of a sudden you feel like you are up against the wall. At that moment you can feel there is a fundamental internal change that is being called for. That's why everybody's life—as it is, if they just let go of seeking to avoid it—is actually the perfect avenue for their own spiritual unfolding. It doesn't matter if you're right here in Palo Alto working at IBM, or being a monk in a monastery somewhere. No matter where you are and what situation you're moving in, you still have the same fundamental question. And it doesn't matter what you're doing, it's what you're being.

Student: So when you say it's about who I am, what happens when the "I" ceases, when you realize that all you know as "I" is not really permanent?

Adyashanti: You find out. I mean you run into this amazingly beautiful paradox that there is no "I" at all and "I" is everywhere, and both of those are true simultaneously. It's about as much fun as you could possibly have. There isn't an "I," and the only thing that exists is one big "I" shining out of everything. But that's just talk. It is also part of integrity to never be satisfied with anybody else's truth. You want to know in yourself because that's the only way that you will ever know for yourself. Independently discover what you are.

There is a mystery right here, even on the level of experience. Even at the beginning you can taste, in the midst of that mystery, a kind of intuitive experience that no separate self is there. You can't find who you are, and yet you are obviously here because there is a perception of this nothing. You can actually get a foretaste right from the beginning that people who have sat on their meditation cushions for twenty years may not have. They can miss something this simple. The taste of it is already with everybody. That's the amazing thing about it. It's not a far off thing.

Palo Alto, California: August 8, 2002

CHAPTER SIXTEEN

LETTING GO

There is a very simple secret to being happy. Just let go of your demand on this moment. Any time you have a demand on the moment to give you something or remove something, there is suffering. Your demands keep you chained to the dream state of the conditioned mind. The problem is that when there is a demand, you completely miss what is now.

Letting go applies to the highest sacred demand, and even to the demand for love. If you demand in some subtle way to be loved, even if you get love, it is never enough. In the next moment, the demand reasserts itself, and you need to be loved again. But as soon as you let go, there is knowing in that instant that there is love here already. The mind is afraid to let go of its demand because the mind thinks that if it lets go, it is not going to get what it wants—as if demanding works. This is not the way things work. Stop chasing peace and stop chasing love, and your heart becomes full. Stop trying to be a better person, and you are a better person. Stop trying to forgive, and forgiveness happens. Stop and be still.

Sudden realization is just dropping every demand on this moment, on yourself, and on others. All it takes is just to drop it for a split second. It's very simple if you do that indefinitely. But if you have a transcendent moment and then start to make demands on yourself and the world, you become confused again because the true nature of being is obscured. It is as if you start chasing the jewel that is in your own pocket and insist that you are a beggar. When you stop insisting and put your hand back in your pocket, you realize there is such fullness *now*, and the fullness doesn't come as the result of anything.

The beauty of Self is that it's not a matter of acquiring anything, being held in high regard, or being seen or noticed. It's a matter of being the intrinsic beauty of what you are, that inner blessedness. To experience that deeply, just let it sink in, not as an answer but as a question.

"Could it be that this blessedness is what I am? Could I have been mistaken all along by defining myself as worthy or unworthy or as the social roles that are played in my life? Have I been mistaken and overlooked the hidden blessedness that is in the nature of each and every being?"

This blessedness seems hidden because it cannot be touched, but it is not hidden in essence. It is overlooked because we are looking only at the mind structure, and we are missing what makes the structure possible. Our structures of belief, disbelief, emotions—all of our inner and outer structures come and go. Only the space that is awake remains. And there is a lot more space in you than there is structure.

What you are is the only thing that you cannot acquire. That's the beauty of it. You can acquire everything but God. You can't acquire God. All you can do is stop lying and realize that you *are* God. This has been dramatized in the past as the death of the ego, which is to give it so much drama as to make it ridiculous. The ego is simply that movement of mind that is always trying to acquire something—love or God, money or a new toy. It is always thinking something is going to make it happy.

The only thing ego cannot acquire is the true nature of what you are. It can acquire a hundred thousand spiritual experiences, but it cannot acquire who you are. The essence of this moment cannot be acquired because it is the only thing that is going on. That is why seeing it is called realization. You are realizing what always is, always was, and always will be. Anyone who has ever had a glimmer of awakening finds this such a shock because you realize you always had what you were trying to acquire all your life.

It's like being a street person who finds a jewel in his pocket. Perhaps he didn't take the time to put his hand in his pocket because he was always putting it in someone else's pocket. This happens spiritually when we put our minds or our hands in the guru's pocket. We notice the diamond in his or her pocket and love to be with it. This is only useful if you listen to the pointing that says, "Look in your pocket, too. Look inside of you and see if you don't see the exact same gem."

You have to be ready. There has to be a readiness to be done with the game of putting your hand in someone else's pocket. Otherwise you can look directly into that part of your being now and say, "Oh, that's nice," but then you'll keep on seeking somebody else's diamond. I meet lots of people who realize who they are to some extent, and yet they are not ready to stop. You need to be willing to stop playing your familiar role. Whether you chase after love, money, or enlightenment itself, that becomes your identity and how you know who you are in this world. If you aren't ready to lay that down, even when you find the most precious jewel of being, you'll sacrifice this precious jewel for the old familiar feeling.

How many people have stayed in a rotten relationship a little too long, knowing it wasn't working but not knowing who they would be if they left it? This tendency operates everywhere in life with such thoughts as, "I'll keep this job—I hate it, but I'll keep it." Or, "I'm the one who keeps pursuing something, and what would I do if I wasn't doing that?" This is a very pervasive game that human beings play to avoid stepping into their true selves. You are an incredible mystery that you will never figure out. To be this mystery consciously is the greatest joy.

To be ready to step off the wheel of becoming is as important as realizing who and what you are. You will be happy and liberated, but your game will be gone. For some period of time, you may not know how to talk to people or what to do, and your life may become unfamiliar. This is a very mysterious way to be. My teacher used to say that when you really realize what you are, you're like a baby Buddha. You don't just pop out of the womb knowing what to be when you've been so busy being someone else. It's like taking your first wobbly steps. But you have to be willing to be wobbly and have some insecurity because, if you're not willing to be insecure, you're going to go right back to the old forms of self-protection and seeking.

It is very strange to be a lover of what is. It is familiar to be a lover of some things and not other things. But when you have this new experience of loving just what is, it is also strangely familiar. It's like a sense of knowing that it has always been this way. It seems very ancient, yet also just born.

In times past, there were monasteries—socially recognized institutions where baby Buddhas could find their legs. Those were protected places where there were people who understood what was going on. Today lots of beings are waking up, more than we can throw into the monasteries. It's getting quite out of hand. And part of that getting out of hand is not having the tight-knit, protected, sacred community to support that newness and tell you not to worry because, in time, it will all become clear. In our societies, soon after the awakening of the newborn sacred being, the alarm goes off at 7 a.m., and it's time to go to work. This is a little bit disorienting. Yet that is how it is. That's what we've got. So it is important to have a willingness to let it be as it is. Nothing hides realization again so fast as trying to figure it out.

It is powerful to experience the realization of our beingness and then to be able to experience that with more and more depth. There is a natural maturing of how this realization functions in the world of time and space, but it doesn't present itself all at once. What is needed is total trust in its maturing, the way we trust that babies become children, and children become adolescents, and adolescents become adults.

Berkeley, California: May 27, 2001

CHAPTER SEVENTEEN

COMPASSION

There are two different kinds of suffering. The first is natural pain. This is the pain of being hungry, physically threatened, or in the natural state of psychological suffering that occurs when losing a loved one. These are unavoidable kinds of suffering. It is easy to talk about compassion on this level. If people are hungry, they need food; if they are suffering psychologically, sometimes they need space for the unfolding of that suffering. Offering that space can be a very deep act of compassion, whether it is given from one to the other or given to oneself. I call this basic level of suffering just "pain," and it can be met in practical ways. Meister Eckhart had a wonderful way of putting it: If you are in a state of rapture meditating and your neighbor is hungry and needs a bowl of soup, it would be much more pleasing to God to give your neighbor the soup than to stay in the rapture.

There is joy in these very simple movements of compassion. When we are not awake to our true nature, we may do these things anyway out of some idea of compassion. But when we have literally touched our true nature, we find that it finds joy in meeting the moment of need. When the selfless nature of Self is awakened, we find this nature does not seek to avoid. Period.

Now the second kind of suffering—the other ninety-five to ninety-nine percent—is psychological suffering that is created by inner states of division. This kind of suffering happens because one does not know one's true nature. The hallmark of knowing one's true nature fully is to be undivided. This does not mean that, once enlightened, you will never experience hunger, or if a loved one dies you will not feel grief. You may experience states of mind that are unpleasant, but what you will not feel is the interior fracturing that makes the initial sadness much, much more. That is another layer of suffering that gets added on top of unavoidable pain.

The true Self can't be divided, but the imaginary self can be divided very easily. Most suffering arises out of this divided self, which exists only in your mind. Because it exists only in your mind and you believe it, it sends signals to the rest of the body, and then the rest of the body has an emotional, traumatic, fracturing experience. In Buddhism you hear about the wheel of suffering, called the wheel of *samsara*, which is the suffering that comes out of this interior fracture, this false sense of self. When it arises, it is cyclical, mechanical, and impersonal. It happens whether you want it to or not. It is associated with the world because the world, by and large, operates on the wheel of samsara.

Samsara is a completely mechanical unfolding of conditioning. One person gets triggered and triggers five other people, who each trigger five others, and it keeps moving out, like the spokes of a wheel, until many are affected. Getting off that wheel of samsara means waking up to the fact that the only thing actually on the wheel is a misunderstanding—the idea that I am this being with these feelings and problems. We call it samsara because it's not actually real. It only exists between your ears. In our culture, we make the suffering of samsara noble. It is almost a sacrilege to imagine that who you are is not a problem to be solved. We are never expected to actually hop off this wheel of suffering and wake up from this trance of "me."

Imagine you go to visit a land of Martians, and you see that each Martian has inside its mind an individualized sense of self, with its own story line of "me." But you can clearly see that none of the stories are true. You can see that they could actually remove that whole story—lock, stock, and barrel—and they would be just fine, because the light of awareness is what is actually living the life, and the stories are simply taking this light and fracturing it. Every being is this light of awareness, but everyone believes their stories are who they really are. That is insane. But of course people think it is normal to be caught in their stories because there is a collective agreement that this is normal. Egoic insanity is seen as normal.

You are not any of the stories you believed about yourself. What you are is actually the absence of story. That's why the Buddha said, "There is no self." In the modern vernacular, he might have awakened and said, "There is no story of me." Your sense of a separate, isolated self is the source of all struggle. You have to struggle because you are paying attention to a conglomeration of images and beliefs. You are struggling to maintain that sense of separate self, even while you are struggling to be rid of that sense of separate self. When you stop struggling, you realize there is no separate self. There is actually no self there. So this sense of self is not a noun, but is actually a verb called struggle. And when you struggle, you suffer.

Why do humans struggle? If there was nothing in it for you, you wouldn't do it. This is important to understand because spiritual human beings tend to wonder, "Why can't I just let go of it?" You hang on because you get some perceived benefit from it—you get to have this experience of being me. It's not one hundred percent terrible, and you can get some sense of satisfaction out of it. To the time-bound sense of self, there can be some temporary, great experiences. There are many experiences that a sense of separate self views as very positive. For example, you go to your neighbors and beat them at gin rummy, and you feel totally better when you leave. Or you hit the stock market and for one year you feel wealthy and on top of the world, and then the next year, it's gone. Or you go to your therapist or spiritual teacher and start thinking you are making progress, and there is a sense of getting better. But this is false happiness, not real happiness. False happiness is a trance, an egoic deception.

Freedom, certainly enlightenment, has everything to do with dying to what is. It's very simple. Enlightenment is nothing more than the complete absence of resistance to what is. End of story. What more freedom could there be than the end of any and all resistance and struggle? But to give up struggling against what is, there can't be any holding on to self-image, to points of view, to ideas, or to identities. This is very important because spiritual people often want to give up their sense of identity but hold on to their points of view, how they see the world. But they can't drag these into enlightenment because enlightenment has no point of view. It has no agenda. It has no great demand upon the world or self or other. It has no center. It simply loves.

The imaginary me has a center. It feels everything is happening to *me*. "I am the central plot in the drama of the universe." The imaginary me plays the starring role every second of its existence, even when it dreams. That's what I mean by the center. Everything relates to it, and it thinks all that happens is personal.

But the truth is, there is no center, and everything is just happening. There are lots of points running around in awareness, but there are no centers. There may still be a focal point in each individual body, but that is different than thinking that the focal point is the center of everything. Remember when science thought the earth was the center of the universe and everything revolved around it? We think all of life revolves around us in the same way.

Do you remember when your idea of compassion was to join in someone's illusory story of what was happening? You felt, "I have to support your illusory story so you will support mine, and then we will really feel bonded and closer together." But the level of compassion I'm speaking of means something else. This compassion means a devotion to Truth. And the first movement of this compassion has to be to oneself. The world is full of people who want to be compassionate to everyone else and save the world. But they don't want to take it within themselves because it will remove the center. That is the ultimate compassionate act, to remove the center. Then there is only freedom—the freedom of awakeness, the freedom to be what one already is, which is spirit, instead of the living incarnation of a story. So this devotion to Truth becomes a movement of compassion, not only for ourselves but for others, and we start to see that what we do for ourselves, we automatically do for others.

When you wake up from your story, guess what you realize about everybody else? They are not their story. They are spirit, too. And that spirit is totally independent of their story and your story about them. So you not only lose your center, you lose their center, that box you would put them in. You see they are the same. This is why it is said that enlightenment is never a personal matter. You can't realize you are enlightened and still believe that others aren't. You can't see your true nature without seeing the true nature of everything. It is literally impossible. This is a tremendous act of compassion, an act of love.

There is nothing that engenders surrender more than an act of love. Compassion naturally brings surrender. But as long as we are surrendering just to gain something, that is not surrender. That is the spiritual person's passion—to surrender everything but to expect blissful and total enlightenment in return. That's like saying, "I'm going to give you a dollar if you give me a million in return." True surrender is more like saying, "Please relieve me of my dollar. I really don't want or need it. I want to experience the joy of not having it."

Surrender is to give up our story about ourselves, even our story about how enlightened we are. We see our story doesn't contain any truth. We can't fix it in any way that will make it true. We can't change a fiction into truth. We can make it better or worse, but it is still a fiction. Starting to see that our story is fiction through and through—this is the awakening. "My God, it's been a fiction!" This is freedom. To the ego or imagined me, seeing this is terrible because it is still interested in the fiction. But to awareness, realizing that the whole thing is a fiction is the greatest freedom. Then we start to see what is true.

When awareness removes itself from any fiction about self, life, or others, what is left is truth. You can't say anything about what that is because then it becomes an idea. But to see, perceive, and experience life without any story, so that the bottom falls out of the center, is actually the greatest act of compassion you can do for yourself or others because then you are "self-less." Self-less is actually a literal thing, to be without a center, without a story; it is not the image the mind holds of selfless, which is a romanticized idea about self-sacrifice. Self-less is being *without* a self.

To have no center is not at all what the mind thinks it is. To realize that you already have no center is to realize a very deep and abiding love, a love that's inherent—that's not produced. It is a causeless love. There is no reason to be at peace, but you are. Even when you have no reason to feel good or be happy, you are still at peace. Love always seeks the alleviation of suffering, not through the alleviation of the story, but through the alleviation of the storyteller, which is the illusion of the me.

Notice that any time you come into right now, right now is tremendously simple. You lose all of your agendas to be somewhere else, to be something, or to get somewhere. Right here is totally adequate. You know you are not a problem to be solved, and neither is your neighbor or the world. This is revolutionary for this current state of human consciousness. Can you imagine if you really let it in that you are not a problem to be solved in any way? Imagine you knew that anything that would tell you otherwise is just a movement of thought in the mind that says, "Whatever is, isn't the way it is supposed to be." So the biggest act of compassion starts within. And when the self is no longer seen as a problem, this is called "the peace that surpasses all understanding."

Until you can see, literally, that everybody is the Buddha, then you are not seeing things the way they are. Mother Teresa once said that when she is treating the sick and starving, she is treating Jesus in everyone. This is not a nice spiritual platitude. It is actual concrete reality. The true Christ is in every being. It is the same as saying the Buddha is in everyone. And the only thing that can perceive this is the Christ within. Only the Buddha within perceives Buddha. Only the Oneness within can perceive the Oneness. The me will never perceive Oneness.

Everybody transmits his or her own realization, like a radio broadcast signal, twenty-four hours a day. And everybody receives it. When you realize that your true nature is already free, that it is inherently empty of image, and that it is pure spirit and presence, you will see that it is what everybody else is. Without even thinking about it, you will transmit this. If you think everybody is separate, you will send out that signal, no matter what you do.

With this freedom you start to realize there is no inner and outer because it is all one, and the vision of this is more powerful than anything that I will ever say. I guarantee you that one being who sees the Buddha in you is worth more than reading ten thousand books about the Buddha. One being who actually knows that there is only the Buddha and that nothing else is going on has a more powerful effect than anything else.

The deepest feeling of a compassion that does not seek to alter anything, paradoxically, alters everything. When you touch inside yourself that which is not seeking to alter anything, you've touched upon absolute nonresistance, and this alters your perception of everything. When your conditioning touches that inside which is unconditioned, it alters your conditioning irrevocably. That is the sacred alchemy, and that is compassion.

～

Student: Is the attachment to identity traumatic for everyone?

Adyashanti: Turn on your television or listen to your neighbor. It is always traumatic, a disaster, as long as conditioning is taken to be who you are. It is not that the sense of identity is inherently traumatic. It is the secondary contraction that causes it to be experienced as traumatic. Open the newspaper. That is the story of the individual I, what it is doing every day. It's pure insanity.

It is so important to be more hooked on the truth than on wanting to get rid of identity. You can't be focused on your identity and get rid of it at the same time. Learn to discriminate what is real from what is not real. Most people, when that sense of I arises, move so fast either to get rid of it or indulge it that they don't even see what is true.

Student: What is it like for you?

Adyashanti: The truth is what is most interesting to me. It is the only thing that is interesting. It is always fresh. Everything else is an outrageous bore. To me the only thing that is happening is the truth. There's only one thing going on, and it's always Buddha, always the One. Interest allows you to discriminate what is true from what is not true. That is very different from trying to seek a result. When you are not trying to have a result, it becomes very interesting to see what is true and what is false.

The brain and mind offer a toolbox with tools that are great for getting practical things done. But any thought outside of toolbox-mind is a story that has no truth to it. There is no objective reality to it. Everything that is happening between the ears is not the truth; it's just a story. What are you without your story?

In the land of division, there is always something to know. But in enlightenment there isn't anything to know. Enlightenment is actually a process of unknowing. When you unknow everything in the mind, there is nothing left but Truth. That type of knowing cannot even be spoken of because, if you do, the mind grasps it immediately and makes it its own mental knowing, which is nothing more than a symbolic representation. Truth can never be found in a symbolic representation because that is not a real thing. When we understand this, it cuts off so much wasted time that was spent looking for Truth in the mind.

Berkeley, California: January 14, 2001

CHAPTER EIGHTEEN

FIRE OF TRUTH

When you listen deeply, feel intimately, and allow yourself to experience this moment exactly as it is, the emotional and energetic bodies soften. Take a few minutes now to just listen to and become aware of your surroundings. As you let the sounds become known, also become aware of the scent and the feel of the space around you in and outside of the room so that your feeling sense isn't confined to your skin and bones. Give yourself an opportunity to be open to the environment of sound and a sense of the space outside your body.

Notice that the more you relax, these sounds and experiences penetrate you and flow into you without defense. You will feel yourself softening and opening. Invite yourself into this openness. You may find that the sense of a barrier between the outside world and what's happening inside your skin becomes very transparent, or you may feel as if you can't find the boundary between inside and outside. Experiences of outside noise and what is happening in your body become of the same quality. A feeling in your body isn't really different than the sound of a car driving by or a bird in the trees. A feeling in your body is not really any more yours than the feeling of the space in the room where you sit. Notice that if you begin to take ownership of any experience, this starts to divide the world into inner and outer, mine and theirs, an outside sound and me. But essentially it's all just experience, inside or outside, the same. Not mine and not other than mine.

The presence of stillness opens the body and soaks into you like a sponge, if you allow it. A silent understanding happens that is not in words but is the direct experience of what is. Allow yourself the great gift of not looking for some alternate experience. Without thinking about it, without the movement of a single thought, what is it that experiences this? What is it that experiences?

Recognize that there is *nothing* that experiences this moment, but even that *nothing* is known and experienced. There is something mysterious that knows, something mysterious that experiences in this moment, but you can't say what it is because, when you say what it is, it's not that. It's closer, more immediate. As soon as you think about it, you see it's not that thought. It's before the thought. No description is necessary, so just rest on the edge, on the precipice, on the direct experience, directly feeling as though you do not exist and yet knowing that you do.

One thought about this mystery sets apart heaven and hell. Thought rips the unity into pieces to be analyzed by the mind. But silence unifies. The experience of this moment is present but ungraspable, known but not definable. This that is awake cannot be caught. You can sacrifice that vain attempt to define and grasp it, and instead just let it go. Maybe you are not you after all. Maybe you are this that is awake inside of this very moment of experience. Find a willingness to *be* it, rather than know it. As the body opens, sounds still flow through silence. What in you knows itself as silence? This is undefinable. If you lose your way, listen again to the sounds. They will point back to the silence, which will point back to that which knows both silence and sound. Don't get lost in thought or you miss your life. Just simply relax, and relax, and relax. It's the simplest act of faith and trust.

This awakeness that is awake within you knows itself. The mind does not know it, the body does not know it, and emotions do not know it. This awakeness only knows itself as itself. This truth is simple, beyond all comprehension. It is immediate, before all seeking. It is ever present, displaying itself as every single facet of this experience right now.

You always have two choices. One choice is the familiar one: to sacrifice this mysterious awakeness for something else. The second choice is not to sacrifice this that's awake and present, wherever you happen to be. You can choose not to sacrifice this for the next promise of a better moment, a better event, or a better experience. This is your choice—to be true to what's true or not. And this is the Fire of Truth. This that is awake now, as you, in you, reveals the utter irrelevance of every other argument, whatever that may be. This that is awake to itself renders everything that is not true irrelevant. This silence burns the grasping for anything else and frees the life that you are, to live itself without negotiation. Feel the immediate visceral invitation of this that is awake, to put down everything else. This invitation asks you to cease bargaining with life, with the moment, with yourself, with your teacher, your friend, your mate. Just stop. This fire is unseen and unknown, and yet it burns everything other than itself. This awakeness that is now in the center of this whole experience of being, is it!

Everyone has the choice of what they give their life to. Maybe this choice has never been known before, or maybe this choice has never been made conscious. Now it is. What's important to you? What are you going to give your soul to? I don't care what choice you make, and God doesn't care what choice you make. But you care, and you are the only one who counts.

That which is awake in you hears the sounds and notices the sights that appear when you open your eyes. Don't lose yourself to sights, sounds, and feelings. Open yourself to them fully, but don't move. Stay in the silence and awakeness. This moment-to-moment choice is the Fire of Truth. It does not leave dramatics in its wake. It leaves something unspeakable in its wake that is more satisfying than joy or peace or excitement. At any moment, if you sell out this that is awake, be aware and awake to what you're selling out. Make sure the bargain is what you want it to be. Or you may, by some grace, by some good luck, realize that nothing in you wants to sell out this that is awake anymore, not even for security or for the good opinion of others. It is a real grace to realize this.

It is utterly simple. In a moment, you gain a life free of negotiation and bargaining. This is what the Fire of Truth removes: your negotiation and your bargaining with what is, the desire for anyone or anything to change. You realize that no changes, not even changes in yourself, will make you happier. To receive this gift fully, it must be given to everything and everybody everywhere. This that is awake doesn't want anybody to change or improve at all. That's the fire. That's the ash of the fire. You realize, "A minute ago I wanted you to change, but now I don't. You're fine. Everybody's fine, and everything's fine." What happened? Nobody changed and nobody conformed to your pattern, yet a happiness is there, made more beautiful because they didn't change. It is more beautiful because of the diversity of beings and life. This that's awake is the same for each of us. And everything else is a beautiful, wonderful expression of diversity.

As soon as I want you to change or you want me to change, a dagger is thrust into the very heart of our existence. You feel it immediately, personally, and closely. This is what the Fire of Truth takes out of your hands. Mysteriously, in that releasing, transformational energy is released. Everything is transformed—not only ourselves, but everyone around us. The Fire of Truth transforms you right down to the cells of your body. Not that you care about or intend this. It happens simply because you don't intend it. As soon as we care, transformational energy is boxed back up, and as soon as the mind tries to box this truth, to understand it within its own concepts, it's like dropping a heavy stone on a mirror. The experience is shattering, and instantly you will feel the tension in your mind and body. This transformation requires the deepest humility without any sense of being humble.

So my invitation is to not look past the looking and not move yourself away from that which notices. Do not improve yourself past that which is already whole. And return the favor. That's the saving of the world. Return the favor and see it over there. Wherever over there is—to your left, to your right, behind you, upside down, under your feet. See wholeness there. That's the transformation of everything. If you don't see wholeness in everything around you, that's the continuation of ignorance, the continuation of violence. Don't sacrifice this that is awake.

Don't think it out of existence. Don't bargain it into the periphery of your life.

~

Student: When I watch the news, I feel such an argument, a re-establishing of a point of view. How can I hold this truth in the face of the problems in the world?

Adyashanti: Words are such a small part of what is going on. The Truth can't be put into words. It's really something that's silent and can't be explained. So, too, within ourselves, that which is very powerful and transformative affects the world in a way that our words can't. And no matter what our words are, even if we're saying, "Peace, peace, peace, world peace," or "Feed the hungry, and feed the poor," if that war is raging inside of us, with every word of peace, what's being transmitted is conflict, conflict, conflict. Even though the words don't say conflict, it is unavoidable. Who we are is what we transmit. This is so important.

I find that human beings are terrified of unity because, in this unity, there's nobody separate from the unity who is going to decide or dictate how that unity acts. And the ego knows that in unity, ego is gone. It plays zero part. None. Zip. And the ego says, "Is everything going to be okay? Am I just going to disappear into the closet and not care about anybody or anything and just sit around knowing that it's all the will of God?" Who knows? If unity wants you to sit in a closet, that is what you will do. If it doesn't want you to be involved, that is exactly what will happen. And if it does want you to be involved, you will still have the capacity to be deeply involved in whatever it might be.

Human beings are coming from separation, not unity, in ninety-nine percent of the activities they do, whether they think they are doing something good or bad. When you come from separation, that's all you're transmitting. When you come from unity, you might still be called and be drawn to do the same things you were called to do when you were stuck in separation. The activity may look very similar. You still may be writing senators or flying across the world, but it's so different when it's done from unity. And when it is, you know it is because your sense is, "I don't even know why I'm doing this." That means there's no conflict motivating you anymore. Therefore you can't come up with a reason because everything is okay. And yet, from that, something moves. The mind can't figure out why it would move if it's all okay. That's when you know you're moving from the unity. You're moving from the sense that the world is okay. The world doesn't need you or your message or anything you do, but you are just moving or being moved to do what you do.

Mysteriously, this movement doesn't happen for a reason. It's just the way life happens to move through you. You might be a Gandhi kind of guy or gal who is moved to take some sort of action. Or you might be like Ramana and say, "It's all the will of God, so why get involved?"

The mind always wants to say, "Which one of these is right?" And you usually choose based on your preconceived ideas of which choice is right or which is good for the world. This is a deception. The mind doesn't know. Just as life can be an oak tree, a pond, a rock, a lake, or a car, it can be a very active or a very passive life, all of it coming from the same source. Do you feel that?

Student: I feel it. It's like there's a power inside. And when I heard you say, "It's all okay," there was a sense in me that it is okay, whether or not movement happens because there's peace and acceptance.

Adyashanti: Then life is moving from its own dictates, not a me moving from your agenda. These are so different. When you look at the change that can occur, you can see one person inspiring thousands and tens of thousands. One person (Gandhi) with a single vision kicked the most powerful nation in the world out of India, actually convinced them to leave. Violence couldn't have done that. "You're rotten, you shouldn't be here" wouldn't have done it. The British would still be there. But there is such power in seeing this Truth. Activity flowing from truth has such potential. Every other motivation for movement, for action, is violent.

I think it's a great spiritual practice to turn on the TV and listen to the guy you hate most, the one who triggers you most. When you can see God there, you're getting it. If you have to turn off the TV every time you see the person, and he sends you into skyrocketing anger, you have a lot of waking up to do.

Palo Alto, California: September 22, 2002

CHAPTER NINETEEN

ENLIGHTENMENT

Over the years of giving talks and having discussions with people about freedom, enlightenment, and liberation, I have discovered that most of the people who are seeking enlightenment or liberation have no idea what it is. It is ironic that people who are spending a great amount of their energy, even sacrificing their lives in some cases, by locking themselves up in monasteries, or coming to satsang whenever a new teacher comes into town, and spending all of their extra money on books, weekend seminars, and evenings like this where they ponder spiritual matters intensely, really don't have any idea of what they are after.

This came as a bit of a shock to me when I started to ask people what it is they think enlightenment is. The most honest would usually kind of scratch their heads as it suddenly would dawn on them, "I really don't know. I'm not really sure." And those who weren't quite capable of mustering that much authenticity would usually spit out what somebody else had said, such as, "Well, it's union with the divine." Other people would come up with their own ideas. In modern vernacular, we call those fantasies. "When enlightenment happens it's going to be…" fill in the blank. Usually the expectation is that it's going to be something like an infinitely extended orgasm.

We say in Zen, "If you sit down, shut up, and face a wall long enough, something is going to happen." Many people have done this and then had an enjoyable experience—perhaps a very extended pleasurable state that lasted a few minutes or hours, or perhaps, if they were lucky, throughout a whole retreat. Maybe this feeling lasted only a few seconds in a given meditation before the mind said, "Now if I just extend this experience infinitely through time, that is what freedom is going to be like."

However, my experience of enlightenment was simply the demolition of everything that I thought it was going to be. And I have never met anybody who has truly and authentically awakened to the Truth who has ever said anything other than that. I have never met a single person who has come back and said, "Adya, you know it's pretty much like I thought it would be. They usually come back and say, "This is nothing like anything I thought it would be. And this is nothing like any of the spiritual experiences I have had before in my life, including experiences of bliss, love, union with the divine, or cosmic consciousness."

Again, as we say in Zen, "If you sit down, shut up, and face the wall long enough, then all of these experiences are going to happen to you." And then guess what is going to happen to those experiences? They are going to pass away. Now, most people who actually know this pretend that they don't. Most people who have been through the list of spiritual experiences know that not one of them has lasted because, if it had, they wouldn't still be seeking the next experience. So most people who have been at the game of spirituality long enough know that no experience has lasted.

Nobody wants to face this. Students can hear hundreds or thousands of times that enlightenment is not an experience, and still they bring the concern to satsang, "Adya, what I gain in satsang when I come, I lose when I leave." And I always say, "Of course. It doesn't matter what experience you have, you're going to lose your experience. That's the nature of experience."

It sounds good to say that freedom is that which doesn't come and go, but the only thing the mind can do with that is imagine an endlessly extended experience that doesn't come and go. And then it thinks, "I just haven't come up with the right endlessly extended experience that doesn't come and go. I haven't got it right."

For some reason, and I take absolutely no credit for this whatsoever, while I sat and faced the wall for fifteen years as a Zen student, various experiences occurred. These events included mind-blasting kundalini experiences, mystical union, bliss, and being flooded with divine light and love. Like most people who sit facing a wall, I found these experiences didn't happen nearly as often or last nearly as long as I would have wanted them to. At particular points along the journey, there was a tendency to think, "This is it! This experience is so overwhelmingly pleasurable that this *has* to be it!" My consciousness expanded infinitely wide, and I was pounded with more insights than I could take in. If you want these experiences, there is a prescription for getting them—just sit and face a wall for endless hours a day.

But I received what I found out later was an incredible grace, which was that right in the midst of these most amazing, beautiful experiences, that didn't happen nearly often enough, an annoying little voice would come in every single time and say, "Keep going; this isn't it!" The rest of me would be thinking, "This indeed *is* it because everything about my body and mind is telling me this is it. All signals are go. The pleasure has become so immense that this has to be it." Then the little voice would come in and say, "Don't stop here, this isn't it."

If I had my choice, I probably would have taken that little voice and thrown it out the window because I noticed that other people had these great realizations too, but at least they got to enjoy them for a few days, weeks, and in some cases months, being very convinced that they had arrived. And I rarely got to groove on one of these realizations for more than ten minutes. That doesn't mean it would stop happening immediately. It just means that while it was happening, I knew beyond a shadow of a doubt that this wasn't it, no matter what the experience was. I say this was a tremendous grace because time and time again it pushed me out of the place where I probably would have liked to settle.

If you hold on to any experience, you will experience suffering as soon as it passes. It's amazing that so often this suffering does not get us to move on, but causes us to turn back 180 degrees to look for the experience we lost. So many times this suffering is a complete waste of time because we don't get the lesson that any experience that came and went is not enlightenment, and we try to repeat or sustain it endlessly.

If we are really lucky, either we know right away that a passing experience isn't it, or the experience fades and we don't do the 180-degree turn backwards. We realize that whatever the experience was, it wasn't enlightenment. Because all these experiences are something that are happening to a me, and any experience that happens to a me is bound by time, which simply means it's going to come and go. For me, this was a grace because I saw whatever experience that came down the pike wasn't the enlightenment I was seeking. It shortened my journey immeasurably.

When we talk about seeking enlightenment, which is about the most abused word in the spiritual dictionary, what we are really seeking is the answer to, "What is the

Truth?" That question is an entirely different orientation than, "How can I get that experience?" and "How can I sustain it?" Asking, "What is the Truth?" is a demolition project. Most of spirituality is a construction project. We're ascending and ascending—ideas are ascending, kundalini energy is ascending, consciousness is ascending. It just keeps building, and a person feels, "I'm getting better and better."

But enlightenment is a demolition project. It simply shows you that everything you ever believed was true isn't. Everything you take yourself to be, whatever your self image is—good, bad, or indifferent—you're not that. Whoever you think others are—good, bad, or indifferent—is not true. Whatever you think about God is wrong. You cannot have a true thought about God, so all of your thoughts about God tell you precisely and exactly what the divine is not. Whatever you think the world is tells you exactly and precisely what the world is not. Whatever you think about enlightenment is also precisely and exactly what it's not.

Do you get the flavor of it? It's a removal project. What does it remove? Everything. And unless it's a removal of everything, it's not ultimately liberating. If there is one thing or a single viewpoint that hasn't been removed, then liberation hasn't happened yet.

In the lives of most human beings, everything is about an avoidance of the truth. The truth that we are avoiding is the Truth of emptiness. We don't want to see that we are nothing. We don't want to see that everything we believe is wrong. We don't want to see that what everybody else believes is wrong. We don't want to see that our viewpoint is wrong and that there is no right viewpoint. We don't want to see that everything we think about God is what God is not. We don't want to see what the Buddha meant when he said there is no self.

We would rather quickly insert a positive statement. So instead of seeing that there is no self and that everything the mind holds as true is ultimately empty, our minds will quickly insert something positive like, "I am consciousness," or "All is bliss," or "God is love." We do not want to see that there is a gaping void at the center of our existence.

Throughout the centuries, when spirituality is spoken of in a way that is as close to Truth as the spoken word can possibly come, it is covered up as fast as possible. Even in Zen—which as far as I can see is one of the purer forms of chasing the Buddha's enlightenment experience—there is often an avoidance of the central teaching, which is that there is no self. That's why when you open a magazine, even a Buddhist magazine, you cannot find the central tenet of the teaching. It's not there. Instead, most spiritual writing tells you how to be more compassionate and loving, how to meditate better, count your breaths, say your mantra, or visualize your deity, and on and on. Even in Buddhism, it is often covered up, though it is a little difficult to hide the central tenet of the founder: there is no self. Even if it's not hidden, it's rarely talked about, and when it is, it's kind of dressed up. The real teachings about enlightenment are like a sword blade that swooshes right through whatever direction you were going in. They cut your legs off, and you find yourself nose-down on the floor, bloodied from the fall.

It was said long ago that it's the truth that sets you free, and the most compassionate thing that we can do for anyone, including ourselves, is to tell the truth. What is not liberating is to tell ourselves or tell each other only what we want to hear. That's not compassionate. That's cruelty in a hidden form because it enslaves us to an endless cycle of chasing something that doesn't exist. The Truth might make our minds feel somewhat helpless, but that is the whole point! That's what surrender means. Surrender doesn't mean, "I'm going for the divine, giving everything up, giving my life, my heart, my everything. I'm giving everything up so I will attain the ultimate spiritual goodie." Many of the people who are doing their hundred thousand prostrations around the Himalayas are doing them only because they think it's going to get them the ultimate goodie. Have you ever thought about it? If I didn't think it was going to get me the ultimate goodie, I wouldn't be doing it, for Pete's sake. A hundred thousand prostrations is a real pain in the ass.

Surrender is the same bow down, internally or externally, but made without seeking anything in return. The rest is a game. It's ego. "I'll pretend to be spiritual because it's going to get me something." The truly spiritual is, "I want only the Truth. I'm willing to give up everything that's not the Truth. It doesn't matter whether I like to give it up or I don't like to give it up. It doesn't matter whether it shakes the whole foundation of my being or it doesn't. And it's not that I want the truth as an acquisition that I can hold and possess. It's that I want the Truth, which by its nature has to be that which is not an acquisition." There has to be an absolute release, an absolute letting go, but not for something in return. The absolute letting go is letting go of the one who is letting go. There's nothing in enlightenment for the me.

In one sense, enlightenment is realizing that there is no separate self. We might hear that a hundred thousand times, "There is no separate self." But what happens when we take it inside and seriously consider what it could mean? We would find it means that everything I as a separate self holds as true isn't.

The taste of no separate self is totally liberating. "No separate self" does not mean there is a spiritual experience that goes something like, "I have extended myself infinitely everywhere, and have merged with everything." That's a beautiful, wonderful experience for a separate self to have, but that's not what Oneness is. Oneness is not merging. Merging happens between two and since there is only one, then any experience of merging is one illusion merging with another, as beautiful and wonderful as that experience may be. Even when I experience having merged with the absolute, with the infinite, with God, it simply means that my fictitious self has merged with another fiction. Mystical experiences aren't enlightenment.

Oneness is when there isn't another. Oneness is—there is only *this*. There is no *that* over there, there is only this. And that's all there is. There is only this, and as soon as you say what *this* is, you've just defined what it's not. *This* is only realized in the utter demolition of everything that it's not. Then that awakening is an awakening outside of everything that comes and goes. It is a total waking up outside of time.

This awakening is just like waking up from a dream at night—which is why that metaphor has been used so often throughout the centuries. The dream is as real as this moment. If you think your life is threatened in your dream, you're going to panic just as much as you'll panic if you think your life is threatened right now. But when you wake up in the morning you think, "My goodness, it wasn't really that real." It was real as dreams go. It existed as dreams exist, but it doesn't have the reality we thought it did when we were in the midst of the dream.

Human beings don't know how significant it is to wake up from a dream in the middle of the night. You literally woke up out of a dimension that you took to be just as true as this dimension. It's a cataclysmic change of consciousness. Everything that I thought was true in that dream ends up not being true.

When there is real and authentic spiritual awakening, the impact is exactly the same. I'm not saying this world is or is not a dream—it's pointless to define this world. But I am saying the experience of awakening is exactly like that. It's the experience of, "My God, I took myself to be a human being named so-and-so and I'm not. And it's not that I'm something better or bigger or more expansive or more holy or divine. It means I'm not. Period."

That doesn't mean there is not a body. There is obviously a body. That doesn't mean there is not a mind. There is obviously a mind. That doesn't mean there is not a personality. There is obviously a personality. There is also a sense of self. Enlightened or not, you will have a sense of self. Otherwise consciousness couldn't work in a body. Otherwise someone would call your name, and you would never respond. As far as I can see, every sage throughout time has somehow been able to respond.

Ramana actually put it the opposite way. He said "There is only the Self," which is just, "There is no self," turned upside down. It's the same thing. What is there when there is no self? What do we call that? Ramana decided to call it the Self. But really the Self is what is there when there is no self.

I guarantee that you will have a sense of self after enlightenment. Your body could not operate without a sense of self. So it's a myth that somehow when you get enlightened, you're going to lose your sense of self. It is possible when meditating to temporarily lose your sense of self, so that if somebody called your name you would not turn around. I have seen people in meditation not even be able to get up. In India they call that *nirvikalpa samadhi*. It's a nice experience. Some insight might come out of it. Some insight might not come out of it. You can have the experience called a temporary cessation of the experience of self, but I guarantee that it will be temporary because your body cannot function without a sense of self.

If you really drop into no self, it's outside of time, which means it doesn't last a short period of time, and it doesn't last a long period of time. It is a timeless realization, and if it's not, then you haven't realized it yet. Then, at best, you have had an experience called "I temporarily lost my sense of self," which is not what "no self" means. No self means, with or without the sense of self, that you directly know thoroughly that there is no self, which also means there is no other. There is only one thing going on. Whether you call that one thing God, the divine, consciousness, Buddha nature, emptiness, fullness, leftist, rightist, it doesn't matter. But when there is only one thing going on, there is only one thing going on. There is only emptiness and its infinite display of itself.

Freedom is the ultimate demolition project because it steals everything from you. That's why it's liberating. It steals your argument with yourself because there isn't one. It steals your arguments with others because there aren't any. It steals your argument with the world because there is only *That*. There is only one thing going on, and that is never in argument with itself. Never. Ever. That's why it's so freeing, because you are freed from this endless twoness.

When there is awakening to our true nature, our minds are no longer looking at emptiness because there is no separate somebody to look at it. We realize that the only thing that's ever looking at emptiness is itself. That's another reason why I am not the first to say there are no enlightened individuals, there is only enlightenment. Enlightenment wakes up. Not you or I. You and I are rendered insignificant and nonexistent. Enlightenment wakes up. That's why it is said that everybody is inherently enlightened. But that statement is misleading because it implies that everybody is a separate, special, unique little somebody who is inherently enlightened, and that misses the point. An illusion can't be enlightened. So it's not really true that everybody is enlightened. It's only true that enlightenment is enlightened.

The other part of it is that enlightenment steals everything from you. That's how you can spot enlightenment—whatever body it has happened through is robbed totally blind, and it knows this, but it couldn't care less. It is so happy to be robbed blind, to not have all those points of view, to not believe the opinions of the mind—which will still have some opinions because there is still a body, mind, and personality that will have their ideas—but these are now seen as meaningless. That's when you know something authentic has happened.

I have steered away this evening from talking about many of the positive aspects of enlightenment, but there is no way you could really see the truth and not be giggling in some way for the rest of your life. There is no way that you couldn't just love this world to death, even though you know it's not half as real as you thought it was. There is no way you could not love people a hundred times more, even though you know that they're not what you thought they were. But I don't want to speak too much about that because the mind starts to think it's being handed candy when it's not. It's being handed a sword.

Santa Monica, California: February 8, 2002

CHAPTER TWENTY

IMPLICATIONS

After you awaken from the dream of separateness and realize that you are the source, you need to discover the implications of applying this revelation to your life. When you truly realize there is no other than you, it takes your breath away. All is one and you are the One.

When I first started teaching, I wanted to believe that all someone would have to do is have the awakening experience and off they would go. Now I know there is much more to it. I found that many people do have that essential, experiential awakening to who and what they are, to the absolute, and yet those who have that experience very rarely become free. So of course I started to ask myself why. To awaken into the actual lived experience that you aren't the body, mind, and personality should be freedom, and initially it is very freeing, very liberating, but most people get so carried away with the emotional byproducts of awakening that they miss the true significance of what has happened.

One of the things missed is the revelation of perfect Oneness, the revelation that you are the ultimate source. You can have the experience that you are free because you no longer identify with a mind, body, and personality, but only rarely, other than having a vague sense of Oneness, does the individual have a really clear perception of the perfect unity that is actually inherent in awakening.

It is much like when you have a dream at night and are identified with some character and think you are different from all the others. When you wake up from your dream in the morning, you realize that you are not the character in the dream. You are the dreamer. Everything in the dream came from you. This is a metaphor for spiritual awakening because, when you wake up spiritually, you realize you are not the body-mind. But what is usually missed is that you are the ultimate source of the entire dream. I think this is pretty easy to understand. In one sense, you see that you are not anyone, but in the other, you realize that you are the source of all.

Why is this so important to realize? Because of the implication inherent within awakening, which is where you find all the value of any true spiritual revelation. You are the ultimate source, and everything is perfect unity and everything out there is actually you, equally. So inherent in this revelation of unity is the realization that there is no such thing as an "other." There is no one else because it is all ultimately one's own self.

I've known people who have had this perception, and then the first thing they do is return to living life as if there was an other. They live life as if there is a personal me and a personal you, even though they have experientially glimpsed that this is not true. So, in many cases, experiential understanding is not enough. But can you imagine how it could change your life if you have the revelation that there is no other and you get very curious about the implications? What if you asked, "What does this mean for me for the rest of my life?"

Most humans base their entire life on the idea of self and other, a personal me and you. But with the revelation that there is no other, there is suddenly no such thing as a personal relationship. How does one live with this implication? Fundamentally, what would it mean to actually know and live that there is no other, even when you relate as apparently self and other in the world of appearances? Most people who are interested only in personal enlightenment think, "As long as I'm free, no one can make any demands on me," or "I'll try to teach others how to be enlightened." There is nothing wrong with being personally free. But what if you take the inquiry all the way? How can *you* be free if there is no personal I? Who is there to be enlightened?

One of the most painful experiences I've had in a long time was when I opened up this idea of relationship in satsang and sat back as person after person implied in their questions, "I'm not getting what I want in my relationship," and "I want to know how to have a better relationship." Students asked how I experience relationship. Annie, my wife, told them, "We don't need anything from each other, and we don't use our relationship to work out things because that's not what a relationship is about." This was ignored, and all those questions continued to come up.

Look at the implications of the awareness that there is no other. When you wake up, you wake up out of this "me and you." If you realize what that means, it just takes your breath away. If there is no other, there is no personal relationship. The whole problem with any relationship has to do with one or both people not taking seriously that there is no other. There is no one to get anything from, no one to change, no one to need or to fulfill a need—all of that is a dream. This is how challenging it gets when you do not just seek after a spiritual experience, but endeavor to understand what is inherent in the experience.

The experience of awakening is like a personal experience of the big bang. Its initial revelation was the beginning. It started out as nothing, so the physicists tell us, and then this little blip ultimately became the whole universe. At the beginning, you might have seen this blip and not realized what was inherent in it, and if you turned away from it, you missed everything. If you look into the blip called spiritual awakening, it holds as much potential as the big bang, and more.

Many people ask, "How do I integrate my spirituality into everyday life?" You don't. You can't. How could you integrate it? You can't stuff the infinite into your limited life. Instead, give your life to the divine impulse. There is no integration. There's only realization, and that realization is always a perfect destroyer. It is a destroyer of all sense of separateness, a destroyer of that which is not true. Throw your life into Truth. Don't try to stuff Truth into your life.

Even when you become very serious and endeavor to deepen your realization, seeing more deeply into it, the appearance of a you and an other continues. If you don't fully take your realization into your relationship, it is going to go on more or less as it always has. The pieces may get rearranged, but the relationship may remain based more or less on what you get from each other and how to work things out. When you go deeper to uncover the deepest realization that there is no other, the realization itself rearranges how this dream of appearances operates. The sense of relationship will operate differently because you have truly realized there is no such thing as a personal relationship between a you and a me. It spontaneously reorchestrates how the whole world of relationship works without you making any effort to control it. To make the relationship better, just wake up more. It may or may not change in the way you want it to, but it will change. Wake up more. Because when you are truly awake, things are simply the way they are.

You don't need a teacher to explain the implications of there being no other—you need to do that for yourself.

~

Student: What does it mean to wake up more?

Adyashanti: Many teachers have likened it to when you have a dream at night. You know how it is if you are having a pleasant dream and you kind of wake up but not entirely, and then go back to sleep because you want to dream? So after you roll over and go back to sleep, you then wake up again and realize you were dreaming, but you are groggy and do not even know if you want to be awake. Later in the day, it is more clear, and you are much more awake. Most spiritual seekers, even after a big spiritual awakening, are almost always still groggy. They go back and forth and are not sure they want to be awake because they perceive a whole different world out there. They want to wake up from the bad stuff but continue dreaming about the good stuff. They literally want to go back into sleep in their personal relationship because they know if they really wake up, things might change in unexpected ways.

When you are groggy, there seems to be so much to give up, and there is so much indecision about whether or not to be truly awake. But when you are really awake, you know it is a dream, and you do not want to go back. If you want to be really free, you have to make the effort to completely wake up. You will then lose interest in untruth and only be interested in truth. The dream state of separateness in all its guises will not interest you.

Who is in control of the dream when you dream at night? You are the dreamer, pulling all the strings. All the dream characters are convinced that they are making it happen. But the dreamer is orchestrating the whole thing. When you dream, you forget that. The transcendent dreamer is the one who creates the dream of the world. If you want to be able to function in the world with any grace, you can't forget that. It is a myth that you should let transcendence go in order to go back into the world.

This whole idea of integration and the concept that you can't stay in the transcendent seems to make good sense until we start to examine it for ourselves and ask if it is true. When you look into your own experience and ask how spiritual realization works, you start to realize so much of what we talk about is just ridiculous—it's the blind leading the blind.

This that you look at and call teacher is your own creation, it is your dream, and you are creating it at this moment. If you let yourself become aware, you will become aware that you are creating it and that the separation between the person listening and the one speaking is only appearance. If you are awakened, you have seen this clearly. But the conditioning can pull you back into the dream. This doesn't matter. You have to just keep questioning the dream itself.

Sometimes we get infatuated with an unusual experience, but we miss something deeper, a realization of that which caused it. We need to ask, "Why did I have such a perception?" Question it. Curiosity and inquiry are important. The reason you have a transcendent experience is that you intuitively grasp the Truth, which is simply the way things really are. Spiritually speaking, the question, "What am I?" is the question that goes right to the heart of things.

The infinite intelligence is actually what you are, but you have to be serious enough to find out for yourself what is true. In order to do this, you have to open to the possibility that all you have learned is wrong. Otherwise, how can you discover what actually is? When you become completely open, the Truth becomes the most apparent thing. Spiritual people always think the Truth is hidden from them. It is not hidden. What gets in the way is the *idea* of what it is going to be. Find that place of what *actually* is. There is only the One manifesting as everything. Ponder and meditate on this until you realize it for yourself through and through. Wake up to what you are.

Saratoga, California: 1999, Date Unknown

CHAPTER TWENTY ONE

DHARMIC RELATIONSHIP

One of the valuable lessons I learned from many years sitting in Zen meditation was that in order to be with myself that much, I would have to find myself. To sit quietly and to know only an image of oneself, or an image of the Divine, is to know only misery and endless chatter. We can never be fully comfortable sitting with an image, even if it's a good image. When we sit as our true Self, then we are sitting as no self-image, no self-concept, and no self-idea. We are just sitting as spaciousness. This is the foundation of true relationship because, if we're not in relationship with what we truly are, we certainly will find it impossible to be in true and deep relationship with anybody else.

When we are in relationship as our own radiant emptiness, the relationship is beautiful because we are being what we are. Essentially we are in love with a mystery. Mystery is in love with itself. When this mystery is in relationship with an other, whether the so-called other is the flower, the bird, the wind, the coldness, or a human being, it relates to these as an expression of the same mystery. This is true sacred relationship, when we see that we are really in relationship with the manifestation of the mystery: here as this, here as that, here as him, here as her, here as coldness, here as bitterness, here as sweetness, here as boredom, here as grief, here as happiness, here as confusion, and here as clarity. All is a manifestation of the mystery. The real groundwork of dharmic relationship is relationship with that mystery, with our own self.

When we sit without a demand on this moment, without waiting for the next moment, without waiting to get it—whatever "it" is—when we are not waiting to get enlightened or to get love, peace, or a quiet mind, and when we stop demanding *anything* from ourselves—then the sacred opens up simply because there is no demand being made upon it. True sacred relationship with this moment flowers when we are not asking it to be other than it is. Then the beauty blossoms. But if we ask the smallest thing of this moment, then we start to miss the beauty. Our asking distorts what we are able to see and experience in ourselves.

The mind thinks that to be free, to be liberated or enlightened, means to be wiped clean of all unpleasant experiences, but that's not the way it is. The Divine wouldn't dare defile itself by removing something. That would be like cutting off your arm. But to experience these same emotions or experiences as the mystery, as God, and as the mystery of yourself, is to totally transform them.

See the wholeness of what's actually here, the quality of the timeless as it displays itself through all of experience. Then your own sense of the sacred, known inside of what you are, widens beyond simply pleasurable experiences and becomes the whole spectrum of experience. You start to perceive directly that all of manifestation, no matter what it is, is the flowering of the Divine. If there is confusion, that is God being confused. If there is clarity, that's God being clear. Next you will be able to see God in the dump, in the trash thrown in the gutter, in the street person who hasn't bathed in six months. You start to see the same sacredness everywhere, the same intimate dharmic relationship of the mystery to itself. And so it goes, more and more, deeper and deeper penetration, and into more areas. As you perceive this sacredness in all things, you know you are not who you thought you were. You are an alive, awake mystery that can't be touched or seen.

When this is known, you can be in sacred relationship. If this is not known and you try to *make* your relationships sacred, you are only trying to conform to your idea of what the sacred relationship is, and this is better known as violence. You may do this for a good reason, with good intentions, but if you try to make a relationship sacred, you've missed it. You've missed that it *is* sacred. When you see that a relationship is already sacred, then you are really seeing that it is a manifestation of the mystery itself.

When you see that everything is sacred, you do not lose the ability to make distinctions. You can see where there may be dishonesty in a relationship, where you are not holding the highest integrity, where there is a lack of intimacy, or where the relationship is built upon images, ideas, projections, or demands. Just because it is seen as sacred does not mean you do not also see parts of it that might be ridiculous. These views are not exclusive of each other. God acts funny at times.

To remain as you are (which is simply the light of awakeness) in the midst of relationship is the most challenging thing that a human being can do. Anything that is unmet or unseen will be like a little button with a "push me" sticker on it—and it attracts fingers. That's the beauty of the sacredness. If it's unmet, if it's unconscious, it has a little "push me" button because then it cannot stay unconscious. There it is! Someone pushes it. Boom! Blame. Oh wow! Now blame is conscious. There is the opportunity. But what we usually do is make it unconscious as quickly as possible. So we don't see: "Blame just got pushed. Boy that's been with me a long time. That's in the programming. How interesting! What is that?" Instead, people tend to go into the psychology of it or into an endless series of ideas and philosophies about it. But what *is* it? What is it like to experience blame? By questioning, "What is this?" consciousness is allowed to get inside of it. So you see, there might be blame, but now it is blame that's conscious. If you try to do something with the blame, such as get rid of it, then you are not really with it.

The light of awakeness itself is the deepest transformative agent, and the deepest alchemy takes place in the willingness to stay conscious to our own unconsciousness. When that little button gets pushed something unconscious arises, and the invitation is to stay awake. That's it. Just stay awake, and then the alchemy happens. Just stay awake. Don't do the spiritual thing, like back up fifty steps and witness it from some infinite distance. That's somewhat better than being lost in it, but even that is a subtle form of unconsciousness because it's a subtle form of avoidance or withdrawing awakeness from what is. Awakeness is just here. You don't need to bring it backwards or up or down or behind something to be essentially free of what's arising. It already is free. It doesn't need to back up. Only the little me thinks it needs to back up or get away. And that, too, can be made conscious. "Ah, there is the little me trying to spiritualize, trying to move away from something. Now *that* button is pushed." Now that becomes conscious.

Awakeness is not moving back from, trying to explain trying to fix, or get rid of. Awakeness, when it's allowed to be experienced, is a deep love and caring for what is. Love is always throwing itself into the moment, here and now, fully abandoning itself into now. To be in relationship in this way is simple. It is humble. It is very intimate. Then you can meet another person in a whole different way.

Most relationships start out as unconscious relationships. When the light of awakeness comes to shine inside of that relationship, the unconsciousness within it is going to be revealed. It's very important not to spiritualize it when it gets revealed. Some people want to spiritualize their relationship instead of making it conscious. They want to make it into a spiritualized fantasy in which their partner meets all their spiritual ideas about what relationship could be. They think they know what it's supposed to be like, what it could be like, where it's going to go.

When you ease back from that, you return to something that's very intimate and innocent, where you are finally willing to tell the truth, not to hide, not to force consciousness into some relationship agenda, but to simply let it emerge. Then you never know what it will be like at any moment—how consciousness, awakeness, and love are going to want to emerge. Certainly this can play havoc with relationship, just like the Truth can play havoc with you. When Truth emerges within you, whatever there is inside that is still clinging to untruth is seen in great contrast. And in relationship, when awakeness gets in there and starts to function and move simply because you are no longer holding it back, the Truth and the untruth in it are going to clash, and you will see the incongruence.

That's where the buttons get pushed—not only my button or your button, but now we have a third button called "our button." Every relationship has our buttons because when we come together, it creates this something else called "our." If either one of us or anybody else pushes the our button, the relationship goes "zing!" because the our button just got pushed. This "us" will have its own buttons and its own unconsciousness, which is a product of the merging of the two "me" buttons.

As we allow consciousness in, we stop relating from our fears. Just imagine if nothing you did was based on a feeling of fear or insecurity. It's very telling when we look into our relationships and ask what would happen if we don't do anything based on fear or insecurity. That's a revolution for most people. The more intimate the relationship, the more of a revolution it is. If nothing is done based on fear or insecurity, it's a whole different ballgame. That's what I mean when I say the Truth can play havoc with your relationship, although it can be a very positive havoc.

I find that many people who have had a deep and profound realization of Truth are overwhelmed by the challenge to be what they really are in relationship—out of some fear or insecurity of how that would be received or not received or what that may or may not unleash. It can make you feel very insecure because you don't know what's going to happen if some parts of your life that have been spent in denial of the Truth stop being denied. Very often, instead of facing the insecurity or fear, people just back away from it. So that aspect of relationship becomes an isolated, separated part of life in which consciousness is not allowed to go. As everybody knows, in both the short and the long run, the more conscious you get, the harder it is to maintain division. If you are going to be totally conscious, relating from division is not an option. So it's literally impossible to be fully awake and not be awake everywhere. If you are not fully awake everywhere, it means you haven't come into the fullness of what you are.

When you get a little spiritual experience, it's very easy to subtly one-up someone who you think doesn't have the same experience. As soon as you do this, there is not a real meeting. So how can you meet the unconsciousness in a way that's innocent, where instead of one-upping somebody, you meet eye to eye? We can learn about dharmic relationship by listening to the birds outside, by observing the quality of our listening, the quality of the embrace of the sound, the way that we let the sound in and let ourselves be touched by it. By simply doing this, we become more conscious. We can learn more about dharmic relationship in this than in a hundred books.

When I used to do retreats at Sonoma Zen Center, where it was very quiet, we'd be up at 4:30 a.m. to start sitting. It was beautiful and peaceful that time of the morning. The sun was just starting to light up the air before it would come up on the horizon, and there was the amazing experience of just feeling the whole world waking up, your whole self waking. It felt wonderful. About 6:30 every morning, across the street from the Zen temple, the neighbors woke up. The neighbors had a different idea of how to get ready for the day. So at 6:30 every morning they played Led Zeppelin in full volume. This is when dharmic relationship can be learned. It is easy to stay conscious to the birds, to the pleasantness, to the beautiful manifestation of the Divine, to your own true self—until Jimmy Page starts striking the first power chords. And there it is. There is the invitation. "What is that? And what's my relationship with that?"

What I found was that it was just another sound, and that was perfectly okay. And it was beautiful because it widened my sense of the spiritual. It just was what is. There is God pretending to be a rock star. God wasn't just all the pleasant, good little moments, quiet and serene. This takes the idea of spirituality and rips it right down the center. It says, "Okay, you want to see God? Here is God—all of God. Not just the part you want to see, but all of it."

Then as a final kicker, in at least one of the retreats during the year, on the last day we'd sit all day, and instead of going to bed around 10:00 p.m., we would take a little break, sit three half-hour meditation periods alternating with ten minutes of walking until 11:30, then sit from midnight to 4:00 a.m. in one continuous meditation period, without getting up. So just in case you thought you had achieved *nirvana* at retreat and were hot stuff because your meditations went really well and you felt really good, forget it! After five days or a week, this is going to demolish you. Nobody is going to walk out feeling high and mighty after that. You might be able to at the first part of the retreat, but not at the end.

This kind of sitting wasn't really necessary, but after doing many retreats, I started to see the beauty of it. What a wonderful gift it was to not walk away with some high and mighty spiritual achievement—thinking how nice and serene I was able to remain the whole retreat. What a gift it was to be put right back into innocence. After a while, it was not a defeat at all. It was just feeling, "Oh, here we are again, a room full of fifty people, and after three and a half hours of continuous sitting, we are all just trying to survive. The enlightened and unenlightened alike are trying to survive." The feeling of difficulty or any spiritual idea about myself, high or low, collapsed. In that collapse I found the dropping of the facade was so delicious, so beautiful, so sacred. This was an opportunity to see the Oneness everywhere, in every experience, not as some idea of what it's going to be like. When the idea collapses, the reality of the sacred has an opportunity to emerge. And the real sacred is much more beautiful than the idea—not as dramatic, but much more beautiful.

Dharmic relationship is a relationship that is real. The beautiful is in the real. It's not in the *idea* of the spiritual relationship. It's in the reality of it.

Marin, California: May 12, 2001

CHAPTER TWENTY TWO

ETERNAL NOW

Take a moment
to check and see if you are actually here.

Before there is right and wrong,
we are just here.
Before there is good or bad, or unworthy,
and before there is the sinner or saint,
we are just here.
Just meet here, where silence is—
where the stillness inside dances.
Just here, before knowing something, or not knowing.
Just meet here where all points of view
merge into one point,
and the one point disappears.

Just see if you can meet right now
where you touch the eternal,
and feel the eternal living and dying at each moment.

Just to meet here—
before you were an expert,
before you were a beginner.
To just be here,
where you are what you always will be,
where you will never add anything to this,
or subtract anything.

Meet here, where you want nothing,
and where you are nothing.
The here that is unspeakable.
Where we meet only mystery to mystery,
or we don't meet at all.
Meet here where you find yourself
by not finding yourself.
In this place where quietness is deafening,
and the stillness moves too fast to catch it.

Meet here where you are what you want
and you want what you are
and everything falls away
into radiant emptiness.

There is a wonderful story about a young man who checks into a monastery, full of juice and ready to be enlightened yesterday. He asks the abbot, "How long will it take me to be enlightened?" To which the abbot answers,

"About ten years." The young man says, "Ten years! Why ten years?" The abbot replies, "Oh, twenty years in your case." The man asks, "Why do you say twenty years?" The abbot says, "Oh, I'm sorry. I was mistaken...thirty years."

If you really get it, you realize that to even ask the question gets you ten years. As soon as the thought, "When will I really be free?" comes up, time has just birthed itself into existence. And with this birth of time you have to think, "Probably at least ten years, maybe forever." Where can you go in order to get here? Any step takes you somewhere else.

This is surprising to the mind because the mind always thinks of freedom, or enlightenment, as some sort of accumulation, and of course there is nothing to accumulate. It's about realizing what you are, what you have always been. This realization is outside of time because it's now or never.

As soon as your idea of enlightenment becomes time-bound, it's always about the next moment. You may have a deep spiritual experience and then ask, "How long will I sustain this experience?" As long as you insist on the question, you remain time-bound. If you are still interested in time and the spiritual accumulations you can have in time, you will get a time-bound experience. The mind is acting as if what you are looking for isn't already present right now. Now is outside of time. There is no time, and the paradox is that the only thing that keeps you from seeing the eternal is that your mind is stuck in time. So you miss what's actually here.

Have you ever felt that you really didn't like being here very much and that you wanted some wonderful eternal experience? That's what is often thought but not said when the teacher says, "Be here right now." Inside you are feeling, "I am here, and I don't like being here. I want to be there, where enlightenment is." If you have a really true teacher, you will be told that you are mistaken, that you have never been here. You've always been in time, therefore, you have never actually shown up here. Your body was here, but the rest of you went somewhere else. Your body has been going through this thing called "life," but your head has been going through this thing called "my fantasy about life" or "my big story about life." You've been caught in an interpretation about life, so you have never really been here.

Here is the Promised Land. The eternal is here. Have you ever noticed that you have never left here, except in your mind? When you remember the past, you are not actually in the past. Your remembering is happening here. When you think about the future, that future projection is completely here. And when you get to the future, it's here. It's no longer the future.

To be here, all you have to do is let go of who you think you are. That's all! And then you realize, "I'm here." Here is where thoughts aren't believed. Every time you come here, you are nothing. Radiantly nothing. Absolutely and eternally zero. Emptiness that is awake. Emptiness that is full. Emptiness that is everything.

You only want various things because you do not know who you are. But as soon as you come back to yourself, to that empty awakeness, then you realize there is nothing more you want because you *are* what you want.

The freedom that's discovered isn't, "I have attained enlightenment." The freedom is, "My God, there is nobody here to be enlightened. Therefore, there is nobody there to be unenlightened." That's the light. Only the concept "me" thinks it needs enlightenment, freedom, liberation, and emancipation. It thinks it needs to find God or get a Ferrari—it's all the same thing when you get right down to it. But in a moment of seeing through the conceptual me and realizing it is just mind activity, you know there is nobody to be enlightened.

Me, me, me. I think this. I think that. I'm worthy. I got it. I don't got it. I'm enlightened. I lost it—this is all mind stuff. There is nobody to gain enlightenment and nobody to lose it. This whole thing has been a fiction. Have you ever felt that your life was like a cheap novel? Like a Nancy Drew series in which, after one story was told and you thought that was going to be the end of it, you found out the author had just spit out another one, and as soon as you finish that one, a new story comes along. But you never find the author in the book. The author never gives himself up and always remains outside of the book.

The mind is like that. After many stories, the little character in the mind says, "I need to be enlightened. I need to find the source. I need to find God. I need to be liberated. I need to be beyond life and death." And then at some point it realizes, "Oh, that's the story!" and wonders, "Who am I without the story?" You put down the book called, "My Life." You see that there is no story and there is no me. The me *is* a story. The whole story springs spontaneously out of nothing, out of spirit, for its own enjoyment. It exists for you to read it—laugh a little, cry a little, have ups, have downs, have lives, have deaths, have friends, have enemies—but never to be taken seriously.

If you have spiritual experiences, that's a great plot line. They show up in most spiritual novels called "My Life." The character is given experiences, gets closer to enlightenment, gets farther away, finds bliss, and loses bliss. Chapter 22: "An incredible insight!" Chapter 23: "The total loss of the insight." And it goes on. You get three-quarters of the way through the series (that's like the advanced soul, right?), and now you have taken on a spiritual role. In the first couple of books, you were just a mundane ordinary person. As you proceed to become an advanced soul late in the series, you have now become a spiritual seeker. You must be getting somewhere. That's what the me does, doesn't it? It looks for freedom within the story, until it realizes the one looking for the freedom is only a character in the story, too.

Then all of a sudden, "What am I? Who am I without any story?" The story spontaneously stops, and there is no answer in the mind because that would be more story. That would be the next chapter. But when you step out of the story, there are no words anymore. You are off the page. There is just awareness outside of the story. But don't worry. The story will go on. It keeps going, even without the me. Movement continues.

When you enter the stillness of the eternal now by letting go of the fictional me, you see that reality, enlightenment, or God is like a flame. It's alive, ever moving, and ever dancing—the flame is always here. But the flame is impermanent. There is nothing about a flame that is permanent, static, or stable. If it were, it would be dead. Reality is alive, ever on the move, like a flame that leaps up from the log into the air. Truth is continuous movement. This movement, this aliveness of Truth, is constant. It never ceases. It is timeless. Impermanence is the only continuous thing, the only permanent thing.

Total stillness of being comes when all resistance to movement, impermanence, aliveness, and change is absent. When all resistance is absent, there is complete stillness, an alive and vital stillness. It is totally still but in endless motion. It seems still, and it seems not to be moving only because there is no resistance. Imagine that you are in a train whirling down the track a hundred miles an hour. On this train there is no wind resistance, so you can't hear the wind on the train, no resistance between the wheels and the track or between the springs that the train rides on, so you can't feel the slightest vibration of resistance. You can see that even though you are moving very fast, inside the train it is absolutely still and it feels as if you aren't moving at all. The stillness of being is just that way. What we call permanence is endless, resistanceless motion.

To have some sense of this is so important, whether you understand it or not, because otherwise you may come to a retreat like this one and miss the point. Maybe you experience some stillness and the beauty, insight, or freedom that comes from this experience. But if you think of it as something static, as if maybe this time you can take it home, then when you get home and open your hands, you will find the stillness is a dead thing. It's a flame, and as soon as you grasp that flame in your hand, it is extinguished. When the aliveness of this moment is experienced free of resistance, it's totally still and it's totally moving, and you can't grab it because grabbing is itself just more movement of the flame. It can't grab itself. It can only be itself.

You can find in this metaphor of the flame so much more. If you look at the tip of a flame, just at the very tip, it's fluttering, dancing all around, giving off a light. All you can see is the source of the light, but light itself is unseen. This light is like the flame of Truth giving off insights, realizations, awakening. Beneath that, the heart of the flame within us is also moving like a flame, undulating like the ocean, not wildly like at the tip. Here in the heart is something deeper even than insight. It's the experience before it becomes an insight. This undulating, moving heart is in union with itself. It's so much in union it's not even moving into some realization, but just enjoying that union and the sweetness, the beautiful love.

Then, beneath the heart is the base of the flame. Have you ever looked at the flame on a log? One night when I was backpacking, I was watching the flame on a log, and I couldn't see where the flame touched the log. Either there was a gap between the flame and the log, or the flame was so pure and colorless that it couldn't be seen. In a similar way, there is an absolute base in the heart where there is emptiness. This is the place before the Truth becomes alive, before it leaps out into existence. And here, even the union of the heart subsides into a ground of being that is so simple. It is that place "where distinction never gazed," as Meister Eckhart called it, where even oneness makes no sense, where the mind of insight has fallen silent, where the heart has fallen silent, and there is just a resting in the simple ground of being.

So this flame of Truth is the *whole* flame with all of its aspects: the wild, the heart, and that simple, simple ground.

Palo Alto and Watsonville, California: 2001

CHAPTER TWENTY THREE

FIDELITY

When you experience the realization of Self, never take it lightly because as soon as your fidelity to Truth wavers, you will find yourself back in separation. If you are not only to taste freedom but to be freedom, you have to have an absolute fidelity to Truth, and you have to be wedded to this fidelity forever. If freedom is going to be a living and ongoing experience, the human part of you has to keep fidelity with Truth and be committed to living that Truth. To be free, the human part has to be committed to Truth forever.

People ask me all the time, "When will it all be over?" and I understand that they are equating freedom with not having to appreciate each moment consciously, not having to put anything of themselves out, not putting in the slightest effort, and so of course the answer is, "Never." This is not to say never relax, but rather to relax appreciatively. We can be relaxed and also open-hearted, available, and really present. When we do this, the implication for how relationship unfolds is profound. What will carry us into living freedom is not the holding of attention so much as the holding of appreciation. We need to not waiver, to never waiver, with our appreciation.

As soon as you break your fidelity to Truth, you kick yourself out of the freedom of Truth. As soon as anything—power, praise, person, place, or thing, outward love, respect, acknowledgement—becomes more important than Truth, you will begin to suffer and feel separate. There is only room for Truth in the Truth. This means there is only room for seeing the Truth, choosing the Truth, and loving the Truth. A fierce commitment to Truth is a moment-to-moment choice.

If you are waiting for this freedom of choice to become choiceless or automatic, you are not taking full responsibility for this freedom—the freedom to choose between Truth and some comfortable story. The fierce fidelity to Truth is not something to be taken lightly. Echoing the third Zen patriarch, one broken vow with the Truth sets heaven and earth infinitely apart. When something distracting comes along and there is a moment where you realize that it's a trance and just the passing of phenomena, but you pretend it is real, that is when heaven and earth go *whoosh*. But heaven can open right back up as soon as you make the choice to tell the truth, as soon as you see, "Oh, this is just the passing of phenomena, or anger, or boredom," with no effort to change it, simply calling it what it is.

It is not enough to keep vows just for the sake of keeping vows. To do so is to break the most sacred vow of all: the vow to love open-heartedly, the vow of the deepest surrender of the heart. Do not make a dry commitment to hold some image or theory of Truth. It is like leaning back in an easy chair and saying to your partner, "I'm not really going to love you, but we'll stay together because I said I would." That is breaking the vow; it might be holding to the letter of some law but it is missing the true meaning, missing the heart, missing love, missing intimacy and vulnerability. It's not enough to do something in a rote manner; your heart and being have to be behind it. Feel this moment, see it with a willingness to experience it deeply, whether it be good, bad, or indifferent. Emotionally and feelingly be fully present, right here, vulnerable, with your heart. Just be present. Don't live from your conditioned mind, live from unconditional truth.

The Truth loves. It does not judge. It holds a big sword in its hands and can ruthlessly discern what is false and what is true, but it does not hold grudges. If you are not telling the truth to yourself, you will suffer. If it was not ruthless, there would be no learning. Truth doesn't spoon feed you. Live by truth or suffer. It's that simple.

When you actually awaken to the Truth, you will see that through every circumstance and experience you have always been loved. It is amazing to see there is a thread of love running through every single moment. There never was a victim, not even for a moment. And even though it may have seemed painful, it was just a fierce sword that was there to get you to really see the Truth. Coming to terms with this is difficult because it steals every thread of victimhood from us.

Truth can dance into existence in many forms, pleasurable and not pleasurable. Behind every experience is love. Commitment to being fully present through all levels of *being* will close the gap between you and what is happening, the gap between you and experience. Kwong Roshi often used to say, "Close the gap, even just a tiny bit, close the gap." Then everything opens up. Close the gap between what is and what you want it to be, between what is presenting itself and what you want to present itself. This gap of judgment is the separation you feel. You need to totally choose what is and lean into it with your whole being.

Now, it's very important to realize you cannot close the gap by your own will, only by willingness. If you try to close it, it becomes wider and wider. But it can close itself when you are willing to surrender to what is. When the gap between "me" and the truth of the moment is closed, the Truth reveals itself as fully present, fully your very Self.

That is what I mean when I say lean into life, into the moment, and into the richness of what is. This is not a lean into transcendental disassociation. It can be if you want, but that's not what I am talking about right now. Go forward into vulnerability and innocence. It's like when you are having a conversation with someone and it starts to hit that magic moment when both of you sort of lean in and are vulnerable with each other. That is where the magic happens.

There are so many ways that the gap can get closed. One way to help the gap close and find stillness is when you are sitting in meditation, just sit. If the body moves in response to the mind, it obscures the stillness. But when the body stays relaxed and still, the mind will start to follow the body, and the gap can close. Then the stillness in the moment can begin to shine. Be conscious of what is causing movement. This is just mind manifesting as body. Be slightly at risk, always slightly vulnerable. Be vulnerable enough to stay awake, to feel the cool breeze fanning the fire of the heart.

The real power is the power of love passionately expressing something very deep inside. It comes from the heart, from overabundance, not from trying to fill a lack. You can feel this spark of life and love through everything in existence. You feel it in the air, in the shape of the flower, the shape of the leaf, the shape of your own body. You can't put your finger on it. It's life, and life transcends being alive. Thoughts die, bodies die, beliefs die, life remains. Life, God, love, manifests in so many ways—as wisdom, clarity, and like a fire burning you to get you moving, to get you to let go and wake up to reality.

When I'm not in satsang, I'm a pretty quiet person. Awakeness can take the form of heart, of play, and of the deepest quiet you can imagine. The common element is the fullness of the emptiness. If we're really available, there is a richness. Even when it is empty and quiet and nothing is going on, there is a fullness.

You are the Dharma. You are life. The flower and the tree are nothing but life. And life is never caught just in its expression. Life will always offer its expressions. So all this comes, comes, comes, comes. It comes out of nothing, just like the flower that's not even there one day and shows up the next. Life expresses itself as a flower, a human, an insight, and losing the insight. But life is not limited to its expression. If the whole world blew up, there would be no less life, just fewer manifestations. Life would still be there. You would still be there. We make such a conceptual deal out of it, but when the earth blows away, life is still there. Like Ramana Maharshi said to his concerned students as he was dying, "They say I am going away, but where could I go?" The flower will die, but life is just fine, thank you. Expression goes, insights go, personalities change, beliefs change. You remain.

Los Gatos, California: June 14, 2000

FOR MORE INFORMATION

For information about attending events with Adyashanti, as well as a complete selection of books, video recordings, and audio tapes by Adyashanti, please visit his website: www.zen-satsang.org

Other books by Adyashanti include:
The Impact of Awakening
My Secret Is Silence

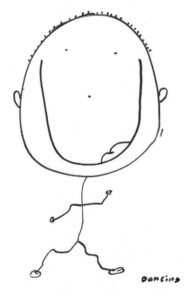

Dancing